AIR FRYER COOKBOOK FOR BEGINNERS#2023

1200 Days of Tasty, Delicious Recipes for Frying, Grilling, and Baking in a Very Short Time

Kiley Arthur Dalton

© Copyright 2022 - All rights reserved.

The content contained within this book may not be reproduced, duplicated, or transmitted without direct written permission from the author or the publisher.
Under no circumstances will any blame or legal responsibility be held against the publisher, or author, for any damages, reparation, or monetary loss due to the information contained within this book. Either directly or indirectly.

Legal Notice:

This book is copyright protected. This book is only for personal use. You cannot amend, distribute, sell, use, quote, or paraphrase any part, or the content within this book, without the consent of the author or publisher.

Disclaimer Notice:

Please note the information contained within this document is for educational and entertainment purposes only. All effort has been executed to present accurate, up-to-date, and reliable, complete information. No warranties of any kind are declared or implied. Readers acknowledge that the author is not engaging in the rendering of legal, financial, medical, or professional advice. The content within this book has been derived from various sources. Please consult a licensed professional before attempting any techniques outlined in this book.

By reading this document, the reader agrees that under no circumstances is the author responsible for any losses, direct or indirect, which are incurred because of the use of the information contained within this document, including, but not limited to, errors, omissions, or inaccuracies.

TABLE OF CONTENTS

INTRODUCTION — 6
- WHAT IS THE AIR FRYER? — 6
- INGREDIENTS YOU CAN COOK IN THE AIR FRYER — 7
- DOES THE AIR FRYER NEED OIL? — 7
- RULES TO NEVER FORGET! — 7
- THE GREATEST BENEFITS OF OWING AN AIR FRYER — 8
- WHAT CAN BE "FRIED" IN THE AIR FRYER? — 9

AIR FRYER COOKING CHART — 10

BREAKFAST — 13
1. Air Fryer Bacon — 13
3. Amazing Breakfast Burger — 13
4. Artichoke Frittata — 13
5. Breakfast Fish Tacos — 14
6. Breakfast Mushroom Quiche — 14
7. Breakfast Pea Tortilla — 14
8. Cheese Air Fried Bake — 15
9. Cheese Sandwich — 15
10. Cheesy Breakfast Bread — 15
11. Cherries Risotto — 15
11. Fast Eggs and Tomatoes — 16
12. Cinnamon and Cream Cheese Oats — 16
13. Dates and Millet Pudding — 16
14. Delicious Breakfast Soufflé — 16
15. Ham Rolls — 16
16. Long Beans Omelet — 17
17. Oatmeal Casserole — 17
18. Onion Frittata — 17
19. Polenta Bites — 18
20. Potato and Leek Frittata — 18
21. Raspberry Rolls — 18
22. Rice, Almonds, and Raisins Pudding — 19
23. Rustic Breakfast — 19
24. Shrimp Frittata — 19
25. Shrimp Sandwiches — 19

LUNCH-DINNER — 21
26. Bacon Pudding — 21
24. Beef Lunch Meatballs — 21
25. Beef Stew — 21
26. Chicken Wings — 22
27. Easy Hot Dogs — 22
28. Fish and Chips — 22
29. Fresh Chicken Mix — 22
30. Lunch Egg Rolls — 22
31. Lunch Fajitas — 23
32. Lunch Pork and Potatoes — 23
33. Macaroni and Cheese — 23
34. Meatballs and Tomato Sauce — 24
35. Pasta Salad — 24
36. Philadelphia Chicken Lunch — 24
37. Scallops and Dill — 25
38. Squash Fritters — 25
39. Steaks and Cabbage — 25
40. Stuffed Meatballs — 25
41. Sweet and Sour Sausage Mix — 25
42. Tuna and Zucchini Tortillas — 26
43. Turkey Breast — 26
44. Turkey Burgers — 26
45. Veggie Toast — 27
46. Avocado Fries — 29
47. Brussels Sprouts and Pomegranate Seeds — 29
48. Brussels Sprouts Side Dish — 29
49. Eggplant Fries — 29
50. Flavored Cauliflower Side Dish — 30
51. Fried Red Cabbage — 30
52. Fried Tomatoes — 30
53. Garlic Beet Wedges — 30
54. Greek Veggie Side Dish — 31
55. Green Beans Side Dish — 31
56. Lemony Artichokes — 31
57. Mushrooms and Sour Cream — 31
58. Onion Rings Side Dish — 31
59. Parmesan Mushrooms — 32
60. Potato Wedges — 32
61. Roasted Parsnips — 32
62. Roasted Peppers — 32
63. Roasted Pumpkin — 33
64. Sweet Potato Fries — 33
65. Veggie Fries — 33
66. Zucchini Croquettes — 33
67. Zucchini Fries — 34

SNACKS & APPETIZERS — 36
68. Apple Chips — 36
69. Banana Snack — 36
70. Beef Jerky Snack — 36
71. Bread Sticks — 36
72. Calamari and Shrimp Snack — 37
73. Cauliflower Bars — 37
74. Cheese Sticks — 37
75. Coconut Chicken Bites — 37
76. Crab Sticks — 38
77. Crispy Fish Sticks — 38
78. Empanadas — 38
79. Fish Nuggets — 38
80. Greek Lamb Meatballs — 39
81. Roasted Bell Pepper Rolls — 39
82. Salmon Meatballs — 39
83. Salmon Party Patties — 39

84. SEAFOOD APPETIZER	40
85. SHRIMP AND CHESTNUT ROLLS	40
86. STUFFED PEPPERS	40
87. SWEET BACON SNACK	40

FISH & SEAFOOD — 43

90. AIR FRIED BRANZINO	43
91. AIR FRIED COD	43
92. ASIAN HALIBUT	43
93. CREAMY SHRIMP AND VEGGIES	44
94. CRUSTED SALMON	44
95. DELICIOUS CATFISH	44
96. DELICIOUS RED SNAPPER	44
97. FISH AND COUSCOUS	45
98. HONEY SEA BASS	45
99. ITALIAN BARRAMUNDI FILLETS AND TOMATO SALSA	45
100. LEMON SOLE AND SWISS CHARD	46
101. LEMONY SABA FISH	46
102. MARINATED SALMON	46
103. SALMON AND AVOCADO SALAD	46
104. SHRIMP AND CRAB MIX	47
105. SNAPPER FILLETS AND VEGGIES	47
106. SPECIAL CATFISH FILLETS	47
107. SQUID AND GUACAMOLE	47
108. STUFFED CALAMARI	48
109. SWORDFISH AND MANGO SALSA	48
110. TILAPIA AND CHIVES SAUCE	48

POULTRY — 51

113. CHEESE CRUSTED CHICKEN	51
114. CHICKEN AND APRICOT SAUCE	51
115. CHICKEN AND ASPARAGUS	51
116. CHICKEN AND CREAMY MUSHROOMS	52
117. CHICKEN AND CREAMY VEGGIE MIX	52
118. CHICKEN AND SPINACH SALAD	52
119. CHICKEN BREASTS AND BBQ CHILI SAUCE	52
120. CHICKEN CACCIATORE	53
121. CHICKEN PARMESAN	53
122. CHINESE DUCK LEGS	53
123. DUCK AND VEGGIES	54
124. DUCK BREASTS AND MANGO MIX	54
125. DUCK BREASTS AND RASPBERRY SAUCE	54
126. DUCK BREASTS ON RED WINE AND ORANGE SAUCE	54
127. EASY CHICKEN THIGHS AND BABY POTATOES	55
128. EASY DUCK BREASTS WITH LEMON	55
129. LEMON CHICKEN	55
130. MARINATED DUCK BREASTS	55
131. PEPPERONI CHICKEN	56
132. TURKEY QUARTERS AND VEGGIES	56
133. TURKEY, PEAS AND MUSHROOMS CASSEROLE	56
134. VEGGIE STUFFED CHICKEN BREASTS	56

MEAT — 59

135. AIR FRIED SAUSAGE AND MUSHROOMS	59
136. AIR FRYER LAMB SHANKS	59
137. BALSAMIC BEEF	59
138. BEEF BRISKET AND ONION SAUCE	59
139. BEEF PATTIES AND MUSHROOM SAUCE	60
140. BEEF ROAST AND WINE SAUCE	60
141. BURGUNDY BEEF MIX	60
142. CREAMY PORK	61
143. CRISPY LAMB	61
144. FENNEL FLAVORED PORK ROAST	61
145. FILET MIGNON AND MUSHROOMS SAUCE	62
146. FLAVORED RIB EYE STEAK	62
147. LAMB AND CREAMY BRUSSELS SPROUTS	62
148. LAMB AND LEMON SAUCE	62
149. LAMB SHANKS AND CARROTS	63
150. MEDITERRANEAN STEAKS AND SCALLOPS	63
151. PORK CHOPS AND ROASTED PEPPERS	63
152. ROASTED PORK BELLY AND APPLE SAUCE	63
153. SHORT RIBS AND BEER SAUCE	64
154. SIMPLE AIR FRIED PORK SHOULDER	64
155. SIRLOIN STEAKS AND PICO DE GALLO	64
156. STUFFED PORK STEAKS	64

VEGETABLES — 67

157. AIR FRIED ASPARAGUS	67
158. AIR FRIED LEEKS	67
159. BALSAMIC ARTICHOKES	67
160. BEETS AND ARUGULA SALAD	67
161. BROCCOLI AND TOMATOES AIR FRIED STEW	68
162. BRUSSELS SPROUTS AND TOMATOES MIX	68
163. EGGPLANT AND GARLIC SAUCE	68
164. EGGPLANT HASH	68
165. FLAVORED AIR FRIED TOMATOES	69
166. FLAVORED FENNEL	69
167. FLAVORED GREEN BEANS	69
168. GARLIC TOMATOES	69
169. GREEN BEANS AND PARMESAN	70
170. HERBED EGGPLANT AND ZUCCHINI MIX	70
171. OKRA AND CORN SALAD	70
172. PEPPERS STUFFED WITH BEEF	70
173. PORTOBELLO MUSHROOMS	70
174. RUTABAGA AND CHERRY TOMATOES MIX	71
175. SPICY CABBAGE	71
176. SPINACH PIE	71
177. SWEET BABY CARROTS DISH	72
179. ZUCCHINI MIX	72

DESSERTS — 74

180. AIR FRIED APPLES	74
181. AIR FRIED BANANAS	74
182. BERRIES MIX	74
183. BLUEBERRY PUDDING	74
184. BROWN BUTTER COOKIES	75
185. CARROT CAKE	75
186. CHOCOLATE AND POMEGRANATE BARS	75
187. CHOCOLATE CAKE	75
188. CINNAMON ROLLS AND CREAM CHEESE DIP	76

189. Cocoa Cake	76
190. Easy Granola	76
191. Figs and Coconut Butter Mix	77
192. Ginger Cheesecake	77
193. Lemon Bars	77
194. Lime Cheesecake	77
195. Macaroons	77
196. Pumpkin Pie	78
197. Simple Cheesecake	78
198. Special Brownies	78
199. Tasty Orange Cookies	78
200. Tomato Cake	79
CONCLUSION	**80**

INTRODUCTION

WHAT IS THE AIR FRYER?

An air fryer looks like an oven because it cooks and roasts. But the difference is that its heating elements are only located on the top, accompanied by a large, powerful fan, which gives extra crispy food in no time. And, most of all, with less oil than frying. Hot air fryers usually warm up quickly and cook food quickly and uniformly, thanks to the combination of a concentrated heat source and the size and location of the blower.

Another great advantage of air frying is the cleaning, as most air fryer baskets and racks go in the dishwasher. Air fryers cook food at high temperatures using a high-power fan, while fryers cook food in an oil tank heated to a specific temperature. Still, an air fryer requires practically no preheating time, while a deep fryer can take up to 10 minutes, even if both cook food quickly. Air fryers require little to no oil, while deep fryers need a lot of oil absorbed by the food. Both appliances offer crispy, juicy food, but don't taste the same, usually because deep-fried foods are coated in batter that cooks differently in an air fryer than in a deep fryer. Beaten foods require little oil to be cooked in an air fryer to become brown and get crispy, while the warm oil dips in the dough in a deep fryer. Flour pasta and wet pasta don't cook well in a deep fryer but do well in an air fryer.

INGREDIENTS YOU CAN COOK IN THE AIR FRYER

Air fryers are *fast*; Air fryers are fast; you can warm frozen foods or cook fresh foods like chicken, steak, pork chops, salmon, and vegetables. Most meats don't need extra oil because they're already so juicy: season them with salt and your favorite herbs and spices. Be sure to respect dry seasonings; less moisture leads to crispier results. If you want to drizzle the meats with barbecue sauce or honey, wait a few minutes.

DOES THE AIR FRYER NEED OIL?

While some recipes don't need oil, most require it even in much smaller amounts than traditional frying. Almost always, 1-2 teaspoons of oil are enough, while for breaded foods, it is preferable to "abound" with 1-2 tablespoons. Generally, just brush it directly onto the food, while you can do this by combining the oil with the breadcrumbs.

RULES TO NEVER FORGET!

Although air frying is a great way to cook healthy food, warm up food or make a quick meal, it helps to learn what not to do. Here is a list of safe fryer tips and suggestions for air frying, do's and don'ts.

1. **READ THE GUIDE PROVIDED WITH YOUR FRYER:** There is precious information on security and how to use it properly.

2. **DO NOT LEAVE THE AIR FRYER PLUGGED IN WHEN NOT IN USE.** Repeat: UNPLUG the fryer when not in use.

3. **DO NOT COOK IN AN UNVENTILATED AREA OR A SMALL, ENCLOSED AREA.** Put your air fryer by the ventilation hoods and turn them on. Keep the fryer away from the wall and open windows as needed.

4. **PREHEAT YOUR AIR FRYER FIRST:** this is a crucial step and is used to ensure even cooking, so don't skip it!

5. **DO NOT BURN YOU AND YOUR COUNTERTOPS:** The air fryer's internal and external components become very hot during cooking. It's easy to get burned, so don't touch those hot items with your bare hands. Use a silicone glove or oven safety mitts.

6. **SPRAY YOUR FOOD TRAY/BASKET WITH OIL BEFORE COOKING:** regardless of the food you want to prepare, grease the basket of the air fryer with a bit of oil so that the food does not stick during cooking. Very little is needed, and a clever trick is to use a spray bottle of oil, which allows you to create a thin film. Oil is also necessary to leave food moist; if you don't use it, dry, tough dishes will come out.

7. **ADD A LITTLE OIL TO YOUR VEGGIES:** You don't need a lot, but a little bit of oil will help your veggies get brown and crispy. You can do this by spraying your veggies with some oil. Frozen veggies turn out better than fresh ones.

8. **ADD SOME WATER TO THE BASKET FOR MEAT:** Adding a little bit of water to the basket underneath the cooking tray, will help prevent excess smoking as your meat is cooking. The grease will drip into the water. It will also make clean-up much easier!

9. **ALWAYS USE THE APPROPRIATE GRILL:** it is located directly in the basket! It allows the hot air to circulate the food and cook food perfectly. The air fryer cooks by convection, creating a vortex of hot air, somewhat like a very powerful small, ventilated oven.

10. **DO NOT OVERLOAD THE FRYING PAN:** Food does not cook uniformly, and air does not circulate properly.

11. **STIR THE FOOD OCCASIONALLY:** to have perfect "frying," stir the food occasionally. It serves to get the heat well everywhere. So, take the basket out at least a couple of times, shake it a bit, and put it back in. When you take the basket out, the machine will automatically stop to start cooking again once inserted again.

12. **DO NOT SEASON FOOD WITH SALT WHEN IN THE AIR FRYER.** Placing dry salt on a non-stick interior may cause the basket lining to decompose and peel. Season the foods in a bowl or cutting board, then add them to the air fryer. Or season after cooking.

13. **CLEAN YOUR AIR FRYER REGULARLY:** If you don't clean your air fryer regularly, it might start smoking, and it will get more and more difficult to clean, which could lead to damage. Always allow the appliance to cool completely before cleaning. Clean the pan and basket with hot water, a little dish soap, and a non-abrasive sponge. Clean other parts of the inside with just hot water and a sponge. You may need to lean the heater element with a stiff cleaning brush to remove food residue.

THE GREATEST BENEFITS OF OWING AN AIR FRYER

There are many advantages to using an air fryer:

1. **HEALTHY COOKING:** With very little oil used in baking, it is the perfect way to replace fried foods that are not very healthy with a healthier alternative

2. **FASTER THAN TRADITIONAL OVEN:** One of the main advantages of an air fryer is that it becomes hot very quickly and the air that circulates helps the food to cook evenly, brown and crisp, without too much intervention from you so that you will reduce your baking time.

3. **AIR FRYING CAN SAVE ENERGY:** when you switch your regular oven on, you have to heat a huge cavernous cooking space. If you're like me, often, you will only be preparing a small amount of food too – resulting in a huge waste of energy. With their relatively small internal cooking space, air fryers heat up much more quickly, have less space to maintain heat, plus cool down quicker. The result is usually less energy used.

4. **GREAT FOR UNIQUELY SMALL KITCHEN SPACE:** for those who might not have a full kitchen's luxury, an air fryer can represent a very flexible and functional way to cook, heat, and reheat.

WHAT CAN BE "FRIED" IN THE AIR FRYER?

You can do all the meals, from breakfast to dessert, with your air fryer.

One of the wonders of Air Fryer is its ability to make anything from essential starters to everyday dishes. Follow the Air Fryer chart with all of the temperatures and cook times. Remember that cook times vary based on the size and quantity of foods placed in the air fryer. You can also open the air fryer during the cooking to check ingredients the fryer heats so fast it won't hinder the cooking process.

MEAT AND POULTRY

You can cook all kinds of meat in an air fryer with delicious results. Remember that meat cooking times depend on the thickness and desired level of doneness. It is always best to use a thermometer to check your meat's temperature at its thickest—You can get meat temperature guide here

SEAFOOD

In order to get crispy, flakey fish, don't overcrowd your fryer basket. The hot air needs to circulate between every seafood piece. Shake the basket every couple of minutes when cooking smaller items like shrimp and calamari, so you get a nice even cook from every angle.

VEGETABLES

Any veggies you cook in the Air Fryer will result in a texture that is most similar to roasting yet is crispier on the outside. Sprinkling a little oil on them before air frying, soft vegetables will cook quickly, while rough and tough roots will take a little longer.

PREPARED FROZEN FOODS

Breaded items like chicken tenders and onion rings will get a satisfyingly airy crunch, while mini pizzas and potstickers will end up with just the right amount of crispness. For any food you need to flip halfway through, grab a pair of silicone-tipped tongs, so you don't scratch the bottom of your fryer.

AIR FRYER COOKING CHART

BEEF	Temperature (°F)	Time (minutes)
Burger (4 oz.)	370°F	16 to 20
Beef Eye Round Roast (4 lbs.)	390°F	45 to 55
Filet Mignon (8 oz.)	400°F	18
Flank Steak (1.5 lbs.)	400°F	12
London Broil (2 lbs)	400°f	20 to 28
Meatballs (1-inch)	380°F	7
Meatballs (3-inch)	380°F	10
Ribeye, bone-in (1-inch. 12 oz.)	400°F	10 to 15
Sirloin steaks (1-inch, 12 oz.)	400°F	9 to 14

PORK AND LAMB	Temperature (°F)	Time (minutes)
Bacon (regular)	400°F	5 to 7
Bacon (thick cut)	400°F	6 to 10
Lamb Loin Chops (1-inch thick)	400°F	8 to 12
Loin (2 lbs)	360°F	55
Pork Chops, bone in (1-inch, 6.5 oz.)	400°F	12
Rack of Lamb (1.5-2 lbs.)	380°F	22
Sausages	380°F	15
Tenderloin (1 lb.)	370°F	15

CHICKEN	Temperature (°F)	Time (minutes)
Breasts, bone in (1.25 lbs)	370°F	25
Breasts, boneless (4 oz.)	380°F	12
Drumsticks (2.5 lbs.)	370°F	20
Game Hen (halved-2 lbs.)	390°F	20
Legs, bone in (1.75 lbs.)	380°F	30
Tenders	360°F	8-10
Thighs, bone in (2 lbs.)	380°F	22
Thighs, boneless (1.5 lbs.)	380°F	18 to 20
Whole Chicken (6.5 lbs.)	360°F	65
Wings (2 lbs.)	400°F	12

FISH AND SEAFOOD	Temperature (°F)	Time (minutes)
Calamari (8 oz.9	400°F	4
Fish Fillet (1-inch, 8 oz.)	400°F	10
Salmon Fillet (6 oz.)	380°F	12
Scallops	400°F	5 to 7
Shrimps	400°F	5
Swordfifh Steak	400°F	10
Tuna Steak	400°F	7 to 10

| VEGETABLES | Temperature (°F) | Time (minutes) |

Asparagus (sliced 1-inch)	400°F	5
Beets (whole)	400°F	40
Broccoli (florets)	400°F	6
Brussels Sprouts (halved)	380°F	15
Carrots (sliced ½-inch)	380°F	15
Cauliflower (florets)	400°F	12
Corn on the Cob	390°F	6
Eggplant (1 ½-inch cubes)	370°F	15
Fennel (quarered)	370°F	15
Green Beans	400°F	5
Kale Leaves	250°F	12
Mushrooms (sliced ¼-inch)	400°F	5
Onions (pearl)	400°F	10
Parsnips (1/2-inch chunks)	380°F	15
Peppers (1-inch chunks)	400°F	15
Potatoes (1-inch chunks)	400°F	15
Potatoes (small baby, 1.5 lbs.)	400°F	15
Potatoes (baked whole)	400°F	40
Squash (1/2-inch chunks)	400°F	12
Sweet Potatoes (baked)	380°F	30 to 35
Tomatoes (cherry)	400°F	4
Tomatoes (halved)	350°F	10
Zucchini (1/2-inch sticks)	400°F	12

FROZEN FOODS	Temperature (°F)	Time (minutes)
Breaded Shrimps	400°F	9
Chicken Nuggets (12 oz.9	400°F	10
Fish Fillets (1/2-inch 10 oz.)	400°F	14
Fish Sticks (10 oz.)	400°F	10
Mozzarella Sticks (11 oz.)	400°F	8
Onion rings (12 oz.)	400°F	8
Pot Stickers (10 oz.)	400°F	8
Thick French Fries (17 oz.)	400°F	18
Thin French Fries (20 oz.)	400°F	14

BREAKFAST

1. Air Fryer Bacon

Preparation time: 6 minutes **Cooking time:** 15 minutes
Servings: 6

Ingredients:
- 1/2 (16 ounces) package of bacon

Directions:
1. Warm the Air Fryer to 390 degrees F. Lay bacon in the Air Fryer basket in a single layer; some overlap is okay. Fry for 8 minutes.
2. Flip and continue cooking until bacon is crisp, about 7 minutes more. Transfer cooked bacon to a plate lined with paper towels to soak up excess grease. Enjoy!

Nutrition: calories 67, fat 5.2, fiber 7, carbs 0.2, protein 4.

2. Air Fried Tomato Breakfast Quiche

Preparation time: 8 minutes **Cooking time:** 30 minutes **Servings:** 1

Ingredients:
- 2 tablespoons yellow onion, chopped
- 2 eggs
- ¼ cup milk
- ½ cup gouda cheese, shredded
- ¼ cup tomatoes, chopped
- Salt and black pepper to the taste
- Cooking spray

Directions:
1. Grease a ramekin with cooking spray.
2. Crack eggs, add onion, milk, cheese, tomatoes, salt and pepper and stir.
3. Add this to your Air Fryer's pan and cook at 340 degrees F for 30 minutes. Serve hot. Enjoy!

Nutrition: calories 241, fat 6, fiber 8, carbs 14, protein 6

3. Amazing Breakfast Burger

Preparation time: 9 minutes Cooking time: 45 minutes
Servings: 4

Ingredients:
- 1 pound beef, ground
- 1 yellow onion, chopped
- 1 teaspoon tomato puree
- 1 teaspoon garlic, minced
- 1 teaspoon mustard
- 1 teaspoon basil, dried
- 1 teaspoon parsley, chopped
- 1 tablespoon cheddar cheese, grated
- Salt and black pepper to the taste
- 4 bread buns for serving

Directions:
1. Mix the beef with onion, tomato puree, mustard, basil, garlic, parsley, cheese, salt and pepper, to taste. Shape 4 burgers out of this mix.
2. Heat your Air Fryer at 400° F, add burgers and cook them for 25 minutes.
3. Reduce temperature to 350° F and bake them for 20 minutes.
4. Arrange them on bread buns and serve. Enjoy!

Nutrition: calories 235, fat 5, fiber 8, carbs 12, protein 5

4. Artichoke Frittata

Preparation time: 12 minutes **Cooking time:** 15 minutes **Servings:** 6

Ingredients:
- 3 canned artichokes hearts, drained and chopped
- 2 tablespoons olive oil
- ½ teaspoon oregano, dried
- Salt and black pepper to the taste
- 6 eggs, whisked

Directions:
1. Mix artichokes with oregano, salt, pepper and eggs in a bowl and whisk.
2. Add the oil and eggs to your Air Fryer's pan, mix and cook at 320° F for 15 minutes.
3. Divide frittata among plates and serve. Enjoy!

Nutrition: calories 137, fat 6, fiber 6, carbs 9, protein 4

5. Breakfast Fish Tacos

Preparation time: 15 minutes **Cooking time:** 13 minutes **Servings:** 4

Ingredients:
- 4 huge tortillas
- 1 red bell pepper, minced
- 1 yellow onion, minced
- a cup of corn
- 4 skinless and boneless white fish filets
- ½ cup of salsa
- A couple of mixed romaine lettuce, spinach and radicchio
- 4 tablespoon Parmesan, grated

Directions:
1. Put the fillets in Air Fryer and cook at 350° F for 6 minutes.
2. In the meantime, heat a skillet over medium-high heat; add bell pepper, onion, corn, stir and cook for 1-2 minutes.
3. Place the tortillas on a work surface, divide the fish fillets, spread salsa on them, divide the mixed and greens vegetables and spread Parmesan on each.
4. Roll up your tacos, put them in the preheated Air Fryer and bake at 350° F for 6 minutes.
5. Divide tacos on plates and serve. Enjoy!

Nutrition: calories 200, fat 3, fiber 7, carbs 9, protein 5

6. Breakfast Mushroom Quiche

Preparation time: 18 minutes **Cooking time:** 13 minutes **Servings:** 4

Ingredients:
- 1 tbsp flour
- 1 tbsp butter, smooth
- 9-inch pie paste
- 2 button mushrooms, minced
- 2 tablespoons ham, minced
- 3 eggs
- 1 small golden onion, chopped
- 1/3 cup heavy cream
- Juust a pinch of nutmeg
- Salt and black pepper to the taste
- ½ tsp thyme, dried
- ¼ cup shredded Swiss cheese

Directions:
1. Sprinkle a work surface with the flour and roll out the tart dough.
2. Press down on the bottom of the pie pan of your Air Fryer.
3. Combine the butter with the mushrooms, ham, onion, eggs, thick cream, salt, pepper, thyme and nutmeg and beat well in a bowl.
4. Add this to the pie crust, spread, sprinkle the Swiss cheese everywhere and place the pie plate in your fryer. Bake the quiche at 400°F for 10 minutes.
5. Slice and serve. Enjoy!

Nutrition: calories 213, fat 4, fiber 6, carbs 7, protein 7

7. Breakfast Pea Tortilla

Preparation time: 14 minutes **Cooking time:** 7 minutes **Servings:** 8

Ingredients:
- ½ pound baby peas
- 4 tablespoons butter
- 1 and ½ cup yogurt
- 8 eggs
- ½ cup mint, chopped
- Salt and black pepper to the taste

Directions:
1. Heat a frying pan that suits your air fryer with the butter on medium-heat, add the peas, stir and bake for a few minutes.
2. Combine half the yogurt with the salt, pepper, eggs and mint in a bowl and whisk thoroughly.
3. Pour it over the peas, throw it away, put it in your air fryer and cook at 350° F for 7 minutes.
4. Divide the remaining yogurt among the tortilla, slice and serve.
5. Enjoy!

Nutrition: calories 193, fat 5, fiber 4, carbs 8, protein 7

8. Cheese Air Fried Bake

Preparation time: 12 minutes **Cooking time:** 20 minutes **Servings:** 4

Ingredients:
- 4 bacon slices, cooked and crumbled
- 2 cups milk
- 2 and ½ cups cheddar cheese, shredded
- 1 pound breakfast sausage, casings removed and chopped
- 2 egg
- ½ teaspoon onion powder
- Salt and black pepper to the taste
- 3 tablespoons parsley, chopped
- Cooking spray

Directions:
1. Mix eggs with milk, cheese, onion powder, salt, pepper and parsley and whisk well.
2. Grease your Air Fryer with cooking spray, heat it at 320 degrees F and add bacon and sausage.
3. Add eggs, mix, spread and cook for 20 minutes.
4. Divide among plates and serve. Enjoy!

Nutrition: calories 214, fat 5, fiber 8, carbs 12, protein 13

9. Cheese Sandwich

Preparation time: 11 minutes **Cooking time:** 8 minutes **Servings:** 1

Ingredients:
- 2 slices of bread
- 2 tsps butter
- 2 slices of cheddar cheese
- A little bit of sweet paprika

Directions:
1. Spread the butter on the bread slices, add the cheddar cheese on one, sprinkle with the paprika, garnish with the other slices of bread.
2. Cut into 2 halves, put them in your air fryer and cook at 370°F for 8 minutes, turning them once, place on a plate and serve. Enjoy!

Nutrition: calories 131, fat 3, fiber 5, carbs 9, protein 3

10. Cheesy Breakfast Bread

Preparation time: 18 minutes **Cooking time:** 9 minutes **Servings:** 3

Ingredients:
- 6 slices of bread
- 5 tbsp butter, melted
- 3 garlic cloves, chopped
- 6 teaspoons sun-dried tomato pesto
- 1 cup shredded mozzarella cheese

Directions:
1. Arrange bread slices on a working surface.
2. Spread butter, divide tomato paste, and garlic and top with grated cheese.
3. Add bread slices to your warmed Air Fryer and cook them at 350° F for 8 minutes.
4. Divide among plates and serve for breakfast.
5. Enjoy!

Nutrition: calories 188, fat 5, fiber 6, carbs 8, protein 3

11. Cherries Risotto

Preparation time: 16 minutes **Cooking time:** 12 minutes **Servings:** 4

Ingredients:
- 1 and ½ cups Arborio rice
- 1 and ½ teaspoons cinnamon powder
- 1/3 cup brown sugar
- A pinch of salt
- 2 tablespoons butter
- 2 apples, cored and sliced
- 1 cup apple juice
- 3 cups milk
- ½ cup cherries, dried

Directions:
1. Heat a frying pan suitable for the air fryer with the butter over medium heat, add the rice, stir and bake for 4-5 minutes.
2. Add the sugar, apples, apple juice, milk, cinnamon and cherries, mix, pour into the fryer and cook at 350° F for 8 minutes.

3. Arrange in bowls and serve.
4. Enjoy!

Nutrition: cal. 163, fat 12, fiber 6, carbs 23, protein 8

11. Fast Eggs and Tomatoes

Preparation time: 7 minutes. **Cooking time:** 10 minutes
Servings: 4
Ingredients:
- 4 eggs
- 2 ounces milk
- 2 tablespoons Parmesan, grated
- Salt and black pepper to the taste
- 8 cherry tomatoes, halved
- Cooking spray

Directions:
1. Grease your Air Fryer with cooking spray and heat it to 200°F.
2. Mix eggs with cheese, milk, salt and pepper in a bowl and whisk.
3. Add this mix to your Air Fryer and cook for 6 minutes.
4. Add tomatoes, cook your scrambled eggs for 3 minutes, divide among plates and serve. Enjoy!

Nutrition: calories 202, fat 4, fiber 7, carbs 12, protein 3

12. Cinnamon and Cream Cheese Oats

Preparation time: 14 minutes **Cooking time:** 25 minutes **Servings:** 4

Ingredients:
- 1 cup steel oats
- 3 cups milk
- 1 tablespoon butter
- ¾ cup raisins
- 1 teaspoon cinnamon powder
- ¼ cup brown sugar
- 2 tablespoons white sugar
- 2 ounces cream cheese, soft

Directions:
1. Heat a frying pan that fits the air fryer with the butter on medium heat, add the oats, stir and grill for 3 minutes.
2. Add milk and raisins, stir, and place in your air fryer and cook at 350° F for 20 minutes.
3. Meanwhile, in a bowl, toss together the cinnamon and brown sugar.
4. Add the white sugar and cream cheese and beat in a second bowl.
5. Arrange the oats in bowls and garnish with cinnamon and cream cheese. Enjoy!

Nutrition: calories 153, fat 6, fiber 6, carbs 25, protein 7

13. Dates and Millet Pudding

Preparation time: 16 minutes **Cooking time:** 17 minutes **Servings:** 4

Ingredients:
- 14 ounces milk
- 7 ounces water
- 2/3 cup millet
- 4 dates pitted
- Honey for serving

Directions:
1. Place the millet in a saucepan suitable for your Air Fryer, add the dates, milk and water, and stir.
2. Transfer to the Air Fryer and cook at 360° F for 15 minutes.
3. Spoon the honey onto the plates and serve for breakfast. Enjoy!

Nutrition: calories 232, fat 6, fiber 6, carbs 18, protein 6

14. Delicious Breakfast Soufflé

Preparation time: 12 minutes **Cooking time:** 8 minutes
Servings: 4

Ingredients:
- 4 eggs, whisked
- 4 tablespoons heavy cream
- A pinch of red chili pepper, crushed
- 2 tablespoons parsley, chopped
- 2 tablespoons chives, chopped
- Salt and black pepper to the taste

Directions:
1. Mix eggs with salt, pepper, heavy cream, red chili pepper, parsley and chives in a bowl, stir well and divide into 4 soufflé dishes.
2. Arrange dishes in your Air Fryer and cook soufflés at 350 degrees F for 8 minutes.
3. Serve them hot. Enjoy!

Nutrition: calories 300, fat 7, fiber 9, carbs 15, protein 6

15. Ham Rolls

Preparation time: 13 minutes **Cooking time:** 12 minutes **Servings:** 4

Ingredients:
- 1 sheet of puff pastry
- 4 handful gruyere cheese, grated
- 4 teaspoons of mustard
- 8 slices of ham, chopped

Directions:
1. Roll the puff pastry over a work surface, divide the cheese, ham and mustard, roll tightly and cut into medium rounds.
2. Put the rolls into the air fryer and bake for 10 minutes at 370°F.
3. Divide the rolls among the dishes. Enjoy!

Nutrition: calories 183, fat 4, fiber 7, carbs 9, protein 8

16. Long Beans Omelet

Preparation time: 15 minutes **Cooking time:** 12 minutes **Servings:** 3

Ingredients:
- ½ teaspoon soy sauce
- 1 tablespoon olive oil
- 3 eggs, whisked
- A pinch of salt and black pepper
- 4 garlic cloves, minced
- 4 long beans, trimmed and sliced

Directions:
1. Combine the eggs with a bit of salt, black pepper, and soy sauce and whisk thoroughly.
2. Heat your air fryer to 320°F, add the oil and garlic, toss, and fry for 1 minute.
3. Add the long beans and eggs, combine, spread, and cook for 10 minutes.
4. Place the omelet on the plates.
5. Enjoy!

Nutrition: calories 203, fat 3, fiber 7, carbs 9, protein 3

17. Oatmeal Casserole

Preparation time: 12 minutes **Cooking time:** 20 minutes **Servings:** 8

Ingredients:
- 2 cups rolled oats
- 1 teaspoon baking powder
- 1/3 cup brown sugar
- 1 teaspoon cinnamon powder
- ½ cup chocolate chips
- 2/3 cup blueberries
- 1 banana, peeled and mashed
- 2 cups milk
- 1 egg
- 2 tablespoons butter
- 1 teaspoon vanilla extract
- Cooking spray

Directions:
1. Mix sugar with baking powder, cinnamon, chocolate chips, blueberries and banana in a bowl and stir. Mix eggs with vanilla extract and butter in another bowl and stir.
2. Heat your Air Fryer at 320 degrees F, grease with cooking spray and add oats on the bottom.
3. Add cinnamon mix and eggs mix, toss and cook for 20 minutes.
4. Stir one more time, divide into bowls and serve for breakfast. Enjoy!

Nutrition: calories 300, fat 4, fiber 7, carbs 12, protein 10

18. Onion Frittata

Preparation time: 8 minutes **Cooking time:** 20 minutes **Servings:** 6

Ingredients:
- 10 eggs, whisked
- 1 tablespoon olive oil
- 1 pound small potatoes, chopped
- 2 yellow onions, chopped
- Salt and black pepper to the taste
- 1-ounce cheddar cheese, grated
- ½ cup sour cream

Directions:
1. Blend the eggs with the potatoes, onions, salt, pepper, cheese, and sour cream and beat well. Grease your Air Fryer stove with the

oil, add the egg mixture, place in Air Fryer and bake for 20 minutes at 320° F.
2. Slice the frittata, place it on the plates and serve.
3. Enjoy!

Nutrition: calories 232, fat 5, fiber 7, carbs 8, protein 4

19. Polenta Bites

Preparation time: 16 minutes **Cooking time:** 20 minutes **Servings:** 4

Ingredients:
For the polenta:
- 1 tablespoon butter
- 1 cup cornmeal
- 3 cups water
- Salt and black pepper to the taste

For the polenta bites:
- 2 tablespoons powdered sugar
- Cooking spray

Directions:
1. In a pan, mix water with cornmeal, butter, salt and pepper, stir, bring to a boil over medium heat, cook for 10 minutes, take off heat, whisk one more time and keep in the fridge until it's cold.
2. Scoop 1 tablespoon of polenta, shape a ball and place it on a working surface.
3. Repeat with the rest of the polenta, arrange all the balls in the cooking basket of your Air Fryer, spray them with cooking spray, cover and cook at 380 degrees F for 8 minutes.
4. Arrange polenta bites on plates, sprinkle sugar all over and serve for breakfast.
5. Enjoy!

Nutrition: calories 231, fat 7, fiber 8, carbs 12, protein 4

20. Potato and Leek Frittata

Preparation time: 13 minutes **Cooking time:** 18 minutes **Servings:** 4

Ingredients:
- 2 gold potatoes, boiled, peeled and chopped
- 2 tablespoons butter
- 2 leeks, sliced
- Salt and black pepper to the taste
- ¼ cup whole milk
- 10 eggs, whisked
- 5 ounces Fromage blanc, crumbled

Directions:
1. Heat a frying pan that suits your air fryer with the butter over medium heat, add the leeks, stir and cook for 4 minutes.
2. Add potatoes, salt, pepper, eggs, cheese and milk, whisk well, cook for one minute more, place in your deep fryer and cook at 350° F for 13 minutes.
3. Slice the frittata, place it on the plates and serve.
4. Enjoy!

Nutrition: calories 271, fat 6, fiber 8, carbs 12, protein 6

21. Raspberry Rolls

Preparation time: 28 minutes **Cooking time:** 20 minutes **Servings:** 6

Ingredients:
- 1 cup milk
- 4 tablespoons butter
- 3 and ¼ cups flour
- 2 teaspoons yeast
- ¼ cup sugar
- 1 egg

For the filling:
- 8 ounces of cream cheese, soft
- 12 ounces raspberries
- 1 teaspoon vanilla extract
- 5 tablespoons sugar
- 1 tablespoon cornstarch
- Zest from 1 lemon, grated

Directions:
1. In a bowl, mix flour with sugar and yeast and stir. Add milk and egg, stir until you obtain a dough, leave it aside to rise for 30 minutes, transfer the dough to a working surface and roll well. Mix cream cheese with sugar, vanilla and lemon zest, stir well in a bowl and spread over the dough.
2. In another bowl, mix raspberries with cornstarch, stir and spread over the cream cheese mixture.
3. Roll your dough, cut them into medium pieces, place them in your Air Fryer, spray them with cooking spray and cook them at 350° F for 30 minutes. Serve your rolls for breakfast.
4. Enjoy!

Nutrition: calories 261, fat 5, fiber 8, carbs 9, protein 6

22. Rice, Almonds, and Raisins Pudding

Preparation time: 5 minutes **Cooking time:** 8 minutes **Servings:** 4

Ingredients:
- 1 cup brown rice
- ½ cup coconut chips
- 1 cup milk
- 2 cups water
- ½ cup maple syrup
- ¼ cup raisins
- ¼ cup almonds
- A pinch of cinnamon powder

Directions:
1. Put the rice in a pan that fits your Air Fryer, add the water, heat up on the stove over medium-high heat, cook until the rice is soft and drain.
2. Add milk, coconut chips, almonds, raisins, cinnamon, and maple syrup, stir well, introduce in Air Fryer and cook at 360° F for 8 minutes.
3. Divide rice pudding into bowls and serve. Enjoy!

Nutrition: calories 251, fat 6, fiber 8, carbs 39, protein 12

23. Rustic Breakfast

Preparation time: 10 minutes **Cooking time:** 13 minutes **Servings:** 4

Ingredients:
- 7 ounces of baby spinach
- 8 chestnuts mushrooms, halved
- 8 tomatoes, halved
- 1 garlic clove, minced
- 4 chipolatas
- 4 bacon slices, chopped
- Salt and black pepper to the taste
- 4 eggs
- Cooking spray

Directions:
1. Grease a cooking pan with the oil and add tomatoes, garlic and mushrooms. Add the bacon and chipolata and spinach and broken eggs at the end.
2. Add salt and pepper, place the skillet in the frying pan and cook for 13 minutes at 350°F. Transfer to plates and serve. Enjoy!

Nutrition: calories 312, fat 6, fiber 8, carbs 15, protein 5

24. Shrimp Frittata

Preparation time: 17 minutes **Cooking time:** 15 minutes **Servings:** 4

Ingredients:
- 4 eggs
- ½ teaspoon basil, dried
- Cooking spray
- Salt and black pepper to the taste
- ½ cup rice, cooked
- ½ cup shrimp, cooked, peeled, deveined and chopped
- ½ cup baby spinach, chopped
- ½ cup Monterey jack cheese, grated

Directions:
1. Mix eggs with salt, pepper and basil in a bowl and whisk.
2. Grease your Air Fryer's pan with cooking spray and add rice, shrimp and spinach.
3. Add eggs, mix, sprinkle cheese all over and cook in your Air Fryer at 350° F for 10 minutes.
4. Divide among plates and serve for breakfast.
5. Enjoy!

Nutrition: calories 162, fat 6, fiber 5, carbs 8, protein 4

25. Shrimp Sandwiches

Preparation time: 12 minutes **Cooking time:** 5 minutes **Servings:** 4

Ingredients:
- 1 and ¼ cups cheddar, shredded
- 6 ounces of canned tiny shrimp, drained
- 3 tablespoons mayonnaise
- 2 tablespoons green onions, chopped
- 4 whole wheat bread slices
- 2 tablespoons butter, soft

Directions:
26. Mix shrimp with cheese, green onion and mayo and stir well.
27. Spread this on half of the bread slices, top with the other bread slices, cut into halves diagonally and spread butter on top.
28. Place sandwiches in the Air Fryer and cook at 350°F for 5 minutes.
29. Divide shrimp sandwiches among plates and serve them for breakfast.
30. Enjoy!

Nutrition: calories 162, fat 3, fiber 7, carbs 12, protein 4

LUNCH-DINNER

26. Bacon Pudding

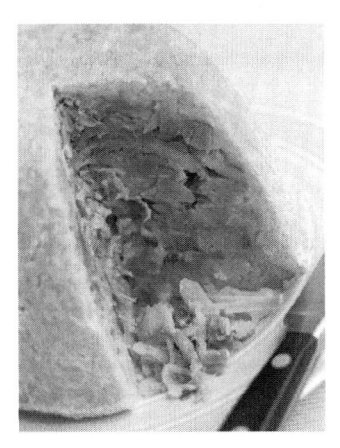

Preparation time: 12 minutes **Cooking time:** 30 minutes **Servings:** 6

Ingredients:
- 4 bacon strips, cooked and chopped
- 1 tablespoon butter, soft
- 2 cups corn
- 1 yellow onion, chopped
- ¼ cup celery, chopped
- ½ cup red bell pepper, chopped
- 1 teaspoon thyme, chopped
- 2 teaspoons garlic, minced
- Salt and black pepper to the taste
- ½ cup heavy cream
- 1 and ½ cups milk
- 3 eggs, whisked
- 3 cups bread, cubed
- 4 tablespoons parmesan, grated
- Cooking spray

Directions:
1. Grease your Air Fryer skillet with cooking spray. In a bowl, combine the bacon with the butter, corn, celery, onion, bell pepper, thyme, garlic, salt and pepper, milk, coarse cream, eggs and bread cubes.
2. Stir, place in a greased saucepan and sprinkle with the cheese. Add this to the preheated Air Fryer at 320°F and cook for 30 minutes. Spoon onto plates and serve hot. Enjoy!

Nutrition: cal. 277, fat 10, fiber 2, carbs 20, protein 10

24. Beef Lunch Meatballs

Preparation time: 13 minutes **Cooking time:** 15 minutes **Servings:** 4

Ingredients:
- ½ pound beef, ground
- ½ pound Italian sausage, chopped
- ½ teaspoon garlic powder
- ½ teaspoon onion powder
- Salt and black pepper to the taste
- ½ cup cheddar cheese, grated
- Mashed potatoes for serving

Directions:
1. Combine beef sausage, garlic powder, onion powder, salt, pepper and cheese.
2. Put the meatballs in your fryer and cook at 370°F for 15 minutes. Serve your dumplings with purée next to them. Enjoy!

Nutrition: calories 334, fat 23, fiber 1, carbs 8, protein 20

25. Beef Stew

Preparation time: 11 minutes **Cooking time:** 20 minutes **Servings:** 4

Ingredients:
- 2 pounds of beef meat, cut into medium chunks
- 2 carrots, chopped
- 4 potatoes, chopped
- Salt and black pepper to the taste
- 1-quart veggie stock
- ½ teaspoon smoked paprika
- Handful thyme, chopped

Directions:
1. In a dish that adapts to your fryer, mix the beef with the carrots, potatoes, broth, salt, pepper, paprika and thyme, and toss.
2. Transfer to the Air Fryer basket and bake at 375°F for 20 minutes. Arrange in bowls and serve.
3. Enjoy!

Nutrition: calories 261, fat 5, fiber 8, carbs 20, protein 22

26. Chicken Wings

Preparation time: 14 minutes **Cooking time:** 45 minutes **Servings:** 4

Ingredients:
- 3 pounds of chicken wings
- ½ cup butter
- 1 tablespoon old bay seasoning
- ¾ cup potato starch
- 1 teaspoon of lemon juice
- Lemon wedges for serving

Directions:
1. Combine the starch, old bay leaf seasoning, and chicken wings in a bowl and mix well. Place the chicken wings in your Air Fryer basket and bake at 360°F for 35 minutes, shaking the fryer occasionally.
2. Raise the temperature to 400°F, cook the chicken wings for 10 minutes, and divide them into plates. Heat a skillet on medium heat; add the butter and melt. Add the lemon juice, toss well, remove the heat, and drizzle with a chicken fillet.
3. Serve them at lunch with lemon wedges beside them. Enjoy!

Nutrition: calories 272, fat 6, fiber 9, carbs 17, protein 19

27. Easy Hot Dogs

Preparation time: 13 minutes **Cooking time:** 7 minutes **Servings:** 2

Ingredients:
- 2 hot dog buns
- 2 hot dogs
- 1 tablespoon Dijon mustard
- 2 tablespoons cheddar cheese, grated

Directions:
1. Put hot dogs in a preheated Air Fryer and cook them at 390°F for 5 minutes.
2. Divide the hot dogs into hot dog buns, spread with mustard and cheese, put everything back in your fryer and cook for 2 minutes more at 390°F.
3. Serve. Enjoy!

Nutrition: calories 212, fat 3, fiber 8, carbs 12, protein 4

28. Fish and Chips

Preparation time: 14 minutes **Cooking time:** 12 minutes **Servings:** 2

Ingredients:
- 2 medium cod fillets, skinless and boneless
- Salt and black pepper to the taste
- ¼ cup buttermilk
- 3 cups kettle chips, cooked

Directions:
1. Mix fish with salt, pepper and buttermilk in a bowl, toss and leave aside for 5 minutes.
2. Put the chips in your robot, smash them and spread them on a plate.
3. Add the fish and strain well on all sides. Place the fish in the fryer basket and cook at 400°F for 120 minutes.
4. Serve hot for lunch. Enjoy!

Nutrition: calories 272, fat 7, fiber 9, carbs 14, protein 4

29. Fresh Chicken Mix

Preparation time: 12 minutes **Cooking time:** 22 minutes **Servings:** 4

Ingredients:
- 2 chicken breasts, skinless, boneless and cubed
- 8 button mushrooms, sliced
- 1 red bell pepper, chopped
- 1 tablespoon olive oil
- ½ teaspoon thyme, dried
- 10 ounces Alfredo sauce
- 6 bread slices
- 2 tablespoons butter, soft

Directions:
1. Mix chicken with mushrooms, bell pepper and oil in your Air Fryer, toss to coat well and cook at 350°F for 15 minutes.
2. Transfer chicken mixture to a bowl, add thyme and Alfredo sauce, toss, return to Air Fryer and cook at 350°F for 4 minutes.
3. Spread butter on bread slices, add it to the fryer, butter side up and cook for 4 minutes more.
4. Arrange toasted bread slices on a platter, top each with chicken mix and serve for lunch. Enjoy

Nutrition: calories 172, fat 4, fiber 9, carbs 12, protein 4

30. Lunch Egg Rolls

Preparation time: 13 minutes **Cooking time:** 15 minutes **Servings:** 4

Ingredients:
- ½ cup mushrooms, chopped
- ½ cup of carrots, grated
- ½ cup zucchini, grated
- 2 green onions, chopped
- 2 tablespoons soy sauce
- 8 egg roll wrappers

- 1 egg, whisked
- 1 tablespoon cornstarch

Directions:
1. Mix carrots with mushrooms, zucchini, green onions and soy sauce in a bowl and stir well.
2. Arrange egg roll wrappers on a working surface, divide the veggie mix on each and roll well.
3. In a bowl, mix cornstarch with egg, whisk well and brush egg rolls with this mix. Seal edges, place all rolls in your preheated Air Fryer and cook them at 370°F for 15 minutes.
4. Arrange them on a platter and serve.
5. Enjoy!

Nutrition: calories 172, fat 6, fiber 6, carbs 8, protein 7

31. Lunch Fajitas

Preparation time: 11 minutes **Cooking time:** 10 minutes **Servings:** 4

Ingredients:
- 1 teaspoon garlic powder
- ¼ teaspoon cumin, ground
- ½ teaspoon chili powder
- Salt and black pepper to the taste
- ¼ teaspoon coriander, ground
- 1 pound of chicken breasts cut into strips
- 1 red bell pepper, sliced
- 1 green bell pepper, sliced
- 1 yellow onion, chopped
- 1 tablespoon lime juice
- Cooking spray
- 4 tortillas, warmed up
- Salsa for serving
- Sour cream for serving
- 1 cup lettuce leaves, torn for serving

Directions:
1. Combine chicken with garlic powder, cumin, chili, salt, pepper, cilantro, lime juice, red pepper, green pepper and onion. Set aside 10 minutes, transfer into your fryer and sprinkle with cooking spray.
2. Toss and cook at 400°F for 10 minutes. Place tortillas on a work surface and spread chicken mixture; add salsa, sour cream and lettuce, wrap and serve. Enjoy!

Nutrition: calories 318, fat 6, fiber 8, carbs 14, protein 4

32. Lunch Pork and Potatoes

Preparation time: 12 minutes **Cooking time:** 25 minutes **Servings:** 2

Ingredients:
- 2 pounds of pork loin
- Salt and black pepper to the taste
- 2 red potatoes, cut into medium wedges
- ½ teaspoon garlic powder
- ½ teaspoon red pepper flakes
- 1 teaspoon parsley, dried
- A drizzle of balsamic vinegar

Directions:
1. In your Air Fryer pan, combine the pork, potatoes, salt, pepper, garlic powder, parsley, vinegar, and pepper flakes, stir and cook at 390°F for 25 minutes.
2. Slice pork, divide it and potatoes among plates and serve.
3. Enjoy!

Nutrition: cal 401, fat 15, fiber 7, carbs 27, protein 20

33. Macaroni and Cheese

Preparation time: 14 minutes **Cooking time:** 30 minutes **Servings:** 3

Ingredients:
- 1 and ½ cups of favorite macaroni
- Cooking spray
- ½ cup heavy cream
- 1 cup chicken stock
- ¾ cup cheddar cheese, shredded
- ½ cup mozzarella cheese, shredded
- ¼ cup Parmesan, shredded
- Salt and black pepper to the taste

Directions:
1. Spray a skillet with the cooking spray, add the macaroni, cream, broth, cheddar, mozzarella and Parmesan, add salt and pepper and mix well.
2. Place the pan into your Air Fryer basket and cook for 30 minutes.
3. Arrange plates and serve.
4. Enjoy!

Nutrition: calories 342, fat 7, fiber 8, carbs 18, protein 4

34. Meatballs and Tomato Sauce

Preparation time: 12 minutes **Cooking time:** 15 minutes **Servings:** 4
Ingredients:
- 1-pound lean beef, ground
- 3 green onions, chopped
- 2 garlic cloves, minced
- 1 egg yolk
- ¼ cup breadcrumbs
- Salt and black pepper to the taste
- 1 tablespoon olive oil
- 16 ounces of tomato sauce
- 2 tablespoons mustard

Directions:
1. Combine the beef with onion, egg yolk, breadcrumbs, garlic, salt and pepper in a bowl, stir well and shape into medium-sized meatballs.
2. Grease the meatballs with the oil, place them in your deep fryer and cook them at 400 °F for 10 minutes.
3. Combine the tomato sauce with the mustard, whisk, add to the dumplings, stir and cook at 400°F for another 5 minutes. Spread the meatballs and sauce on the plates and serve for breakfast.
4. Enjoy!

Nutrition: calories 301, fat 8, fiber 9, carbs 16, protein 5

35. Pasta Salad

Preparation time: 14 minutes **Cooking time:** 15 minutes **Servings:** 6
Ingredients:
- 1 zucchini, halved and coarse chopped
- 1 orange sweet pepper, coarsely chopped
- 1 green pepper, coarsely chopped
- 1 red onion, roughly minced
- 4 ounces brown mushrooms, cut in two
- Salt and black pepper to the taste
- A teaspoon of Italian seasoning
- 1-pound penne rigate, already cooked
- 1 cup cherry tomatoes, halved
- ½ cup kalamata olive pitted and halved
- ¼ cup olive oil
- 3 tablespoons balsamic vinegar
- 2 tablespoons basil, chopped

Directions:
1. Toss zucchini with mushrooms, orange pepper, green pepper, red onion, salt and pepper, Italian seasoning and oil in a bowl.
2. Stir to combine, transfer to air fryer preheated to 380°F and cook for 12 minutes. Combine the pasta with the cooked vegetables, cherry tomatoes, olives, vinegar and basil, stir and serve at noon.
3. Enjoy!

Nutrition: calories 201, fat 5, fiber 9, carbs 11, protein 5

36. Philadelphia Chicken Lunch

Preparation time: 15 minutes **Cooking time:** 32 minutes **Servings:** 4
Ingredients:
- 1 teaspoon olive oil
- 1 yellow onion, sliced
- 2 chicken breasts, skinless, boneless and sliced
- Salt and black pepper to the taste
- 1 tablespoon Worcestershire sauce
- 14 ounces of pizza dough
- 1 and ½ cups cheddar cheese, grated
- ½ cup jarred cheese sauce

Directions:
1. Preheat the air fryer to 400° F, add half of the oil and the onions and fry for 8 minutes, stirring once.
2. Add the chicken chunks, Worcestershire sauce, salt and pepper, mix and sauté in the open air for 8 minutes, stirring once and transfer everything to a bowl.
3. Roll the pizza dough onto a work surface to form a rectangle. Divide the cheese evenly and add the chicken and onion mixture. Garnish with cheese gravy.
4. Roll your dough and make it U-shaped. Put your roll in your fryer basket, brush with the remaining oil and cook at 370°F for 12 minutes, turning the roll halfway.
5. Cut your roll while it is warm and serve.
6. Enjoy!

Nutrition: cal. 301, fat 8, fiber 17, carbs 20, protein 6

37. Scallops and Dill

Preparation time: 13 minutes **Cooking time:** 5 minutes
Servings: 4
Ingredients:
- 1 pound sea scallops, debearded
- 1 tablespoon lemon juice
- 1 teaspoon dill, chopped
- 2 teaspoons olive oil
- Salt and black pepper to the taste

Directions:
1. In your Air Fryer, mix scallops with dill, oil, salt, pepper and lemon juice, cover and cook at 360°F for 5 minutes.
2. Discard unopened ones, divide scallops and dill sauce among plates and serve for lunch. Enjoy!

Nutrition: calories 152, fat 4, fiber 7, carbs 19, protein 4

38. Squash Fritters

Preparation time: 14 minutes **Cooking time:** 7 minutes
Servings: 4
Ingredients:
- 3 ounces of cream cheese
- 1 egg, whisked
- ½ teaspoon oregano, dried
- A pinch of salt and black pepper
- 1 yellow summer squash, grated
- 1/3 cup carrot, grated
- 2/3 cup breadcrumbs
- 2 tablespoons olive oil

Directions:
1. Mix cream cheese with salt, pepper, oregano, egg, breadcrumbs, carrot and squash in a bowl and stir well.
2. Shape medium patties out of this mix and brush them with the oil.
3. Place squash patties in your Air Fryer, cook them at 400°F for 7 minutes.
4. Serve them for lunch. Enjoy!

Nutrition: calories 200, fat 4, fiber 7, carbs 8, protein 6

39. Steaks and Cabbage

Preparation time: 16 minutes **Cooking time:** 10 minutes **Servings:** 4
Ingredients:
- ½ pound sirloin steak, cut into strips
- 2 teaspoons cornstarch
- 1 tablespoon peanut oil
- 2 cups green cabbage, chopped
- 1 yellow bell pepper, chopped
- 2 green onions, chopped
- 2 garlic cloves, minced
- Salt and black pepper to the taste

Directions:
1. Mix cabbage salt, pepper, and peanut oil in a bowl, and toss.
2. Transfer to the Air Fryer basket, bake at 370°F for 4 minutes, then put in a bowl.
3. Add steak strips to your Air Fryer, green onions, red pepper, garlic, salt and pepper, stir and cook for 5 minutes. Add to the cabbage, stir, divide among the dishes and serve at noon.
4. Enjoy!

Nutrition: calories 283, fat 6, fiber 8, carbs 14, protein 6

40. Stuffed Meatballs

Preparation time: 11 minutes **Cooking time:** 10 minutes **Servings:** 4
Ingredients:
- 1/3 cup breadcrumbs
- 3 tablespoons milk
- 1 tablespoon ketchup
- 1 egg
- ½ teaspoon marjoram, dried
- Salt and black pepper to the taste
- 1-pound lean beef, ground
- 20 cheddar cheese cubes
- 1 tablespoon olive oil

Directions:
1. Combine the breadcrumbs with the ketchup, milk, marjoram, salt, pepper and egg and whip well.
2. Add beef, toss and form 20 meatballs. Shape each dumpling around a cheese cube, pour the oil on top and rub.
3. Place all meatballs in the pre-warmed air fryer, cook at 390°F for 10 minutes. Serve them at lunchtime with a side salad.
4. Enjoy!

Nutrition: calories 201, fat 5, fiber 8, carbs 12, protein 5

41. Sweet and Sour Sausage Mix

Preparation time: 12 minutes **Cooking time:** 10 minutes **Servings:** 4
Ingredients:
- 1-pound sausages, sliced
- 1 red bell pepper, cut into strips
- ½ cup yellow onion, chopped
- 3 tablespoons brown sugar

- 1/3 cup ketchup
- 2 tablespoons mustard
- 2 tablespoons apple cider vinegar
- ½ cup chicken stock

Directions:
1. Combine sugar, ketchup, mustard, stock and vinegar and beat well.
2. In your Air Fryer skillet, mix sausage slices with the bell pepper, onion and sweet and sour mixture, stir and cook at 350°F for 10 minutes.
3. Divide among bowls and serve.
4. Enjoy!

Nutrition: calories 163, fat 6, fiber 9, carbs 12, protein 6

42. Tuna and Zucchini Tortillas

Preparation time: 12 minutes **Cooking time:** 10 minutes **Servings:** 4

Ingredients:
- 4 corn tortillas
- 4 tablespoons butter, soft
- 6 ounces canned tuna, drained
- 1 cup zucchini, shredded
- 1/3 cup mayonnaise
- 2 tablespoons mustard
- 1 cup cheddar cheese, grated

Directions:
1. Spread butter on tortillas, place them in your Air Fryer's basket and cook them at 400°F for 3 minutes.
2. Meanwhile, mix tuna with zucchini, mayo and mustard and stir.
3. Divide this mix on each tortilla, top with cheese, roll tortillas, place them in your Air Fryer's basket again and cook them at 400°F for 4 minutes. Serve for lunch.
4. Enjoy!

Nutrition: calories 162, fat 4, fiber 8, carbs 9, protein 4

43. Turkey Breast

Preparation time: 13 minutes **Cooking time:** 47 minutes **Servings:** 4

Ingredients:
- 1 big turkey breast
- 2 teaspoons olive oil
- ½ teaspoon smoked paprika
- 1 teaspoon thyme, dried
- ½ teaspoon sage, dried
- Salt and black pepper to the taste
- 2 tablespoons mustard
- ¼ cup maple syrup
- 1 tablespoon butter, soft

Directions:
1. Baste turkey breast with olive oil, season with salt, pepper, thyme, paprika and sage, rub, place in the frying pan and fry at 350°F for 25 minutes.
2. Turn the turkey, cook for ten more minutes, turn again and cook for another 10 minutes.
3. Meanwhile, heat a pan with the butter over medium heat, add mustard and maple syrup, stir well, cook for a couple of minutes and take off the heat.
4. Slice the turkey breast, divide among the plates and serve with the maple icing watered. Enjoy!

Nutrition: calories 280, fat 2, fiber 7, carbs 16, protein 14

44. Turkey Burgers

Preparation time: 10 minutes **Cooking time:** 8 minutes **Servings:** 4

Ingredients:
- 1 pound of turkey meat, ground
- 1 shallot, minced
- A drizzle of olive oil
- 1 small jalapeño pepper, minced
- 2 teaspoons lime juice
- Zest from 1 lime, grated
- Salt and black pepper to the taste
- 1 teaspoon cumin, ground
- 1 teaspoon sweet paprika
- Guacamole for serving

Directions:
1. Mix turkey meat with salt, pepper, cumin, paprika, shallot, jalapeño, lime juice and zest, stir well, shape burgers from this mix, and drizzle the oil over them.
2. Introduce to preheated Air Fryer and cook them at 370°F for 8 minutes on each side.
3. Divide among plates and serve with guacamole on top. Enjoy!

Nutrition: calories 200, fat 12, fiber 0, carbs 0, protein 12

45. Veggie Toast

Preparation time: 12 minutes **Cooking time:** 15 minutes **Servings:** 4

Ingredients:
- 1 red bell pepper, thinly sliced
- 1 cup cremini mushrooms, sliced
- 1 yellow squash, chopped
- 2 green onions, sliced
- 1 tablespoon olive oil
- 4 bread slices
- 2 tablespoons butter, soft
- ½ cup goat cheese, crumbled

Directions:
1. In a bowl, mix red bell pepper with mushrooms, squash, green onions and oil, toss, and transfer to your Air Fryer.
2. Cook them at 350°F for 10 minutes, shaking the fryer once and transfer them to a bowl.
3. Spread butter on bread slices, place them in Air Fryer and cook them at 350°F for 5 minutes.
4. Divide veggie mix on each bread slice, top with crumbled cheese and serve for lunch. Enjoy!

Nutrition: calories 152, fat 3, fiber 4, carbs 7, protein 2

SIDE DISHES

46. Avocado Fries

Preparation time: 12 minutes **Cooking time:** 10 minutes **Servings:** 4
Ingredients:
- 1 avocado, pitted, peeled, sliced and cut into medium fries
- Salt and black pepper to the taste
- ½ cup panko breadcrumbs
- 1 tablespoon lemon juice
- 1 egg, whisked
- 1 tablespoon olive oil

Directions:
1. In a bowl, mix panko with salt and pepper and stir. Mix the egg with a pinch of salt in another bowl, and whisk.
2. In a third bowl, mix avocado fries with lemon juice and oil and toss.
3. Dip fries in egg, then in panko, place them in your Air Fryer's basket and cook at 390°F for 10 minutes, shaking halfway.
4. Divide among plates and serve as a side dish. Enjoy!

Nutrition: calorie 130, fat 11, fiber 3, carbs 16, protein 4

47. Brussels Sprouts and Pomegranate Seeds

Preparation time: 8 minutes **Cooking time:** 10 minutes **Servings:** 4
Ingredients:
- 1 pound Brussels sprouts, trimmed and halved
- Salt and black pepper to the taste
- 1 cup pomegranate seeds
- ¼ cup of pine nuts, toasted
- 1 tablespoon olive oil
- 2 tablespoons veggie stock

Directions:
1. Mix Brussels sprouts with salt, pepper, pomegranate seeds, pine nuts, oil and stock, and stir in a heat-proof dish that fits your Air Fryer.
2. Place in your Air Fryer's basket and cook at 390°F for 10 minutes.
3. Divide among plates and serve as a side dish. Enjoy!

Nutrition: calories 152, fat 4, fiber 7, carbs 12, protein 3

48. Brussels Sprouts Side Dish

Preparation time: 11 minutes **Cooking time:** 15 minutes **Servings:** 4
Ingredients:
- 1 pound Brussels sprouts, trimmed and halved
- Salt and black pepper to the taste
- 6 teaspoons olive oil
- ½ teaspoon thyme, chopped
- ½ cup mayonnaise
- 2 tablespoons roasted garlic, crushed

Directions:
1. In your Air Fryer, mix Brussels sprouts with salt, pepper and oil, toss well and cook them at 390°F for 15 minutes.
2. Meanwhile, mix thyme with mayo and garlic in a bowl and whisk well.
3. Divide Brussels sprouts on plates, drizzle garlic sauce and serve as a side dish. Enjoy!

Nutrition: calories 172, fat 6, fiber 8, carbs 12, protein 6

49. Eggplant Fries

Preparation time: 13 minutes **Cooking time:** 5 minutes **Servings:** 4
Ingredients:
- Cooking spray
- 1 eggplant, peeled and cut into medium fries
- 2 tablespoons milk
- 1 egg, whisked
- 2 cups panko breadcrumbs
- ½ cup Italian cheese, shredded
- A pinch of salt and black pepper to the taste

Directions:
1. Mix egg with milk, salt and pepper and whisk well.

2. In another bowl, mix panko with cheese and stir.
3. Dip eggplant fries in egg mix, coat in panko mix, place them in your Air Fryer greased with cooking spray and cook at 400°F for 5 minutes.
4. Divide among plates and serve as a side dish. Enjoy!

Nutrition: calories 162, fat 5, fiber 5, carbs 7, protein 6

50. Flavored Cauliflower Side Dish

Preparation time: 12 minutes **Cooking time:** 10 minutes **Servings:** 4
Ingredients:
- 12 cauliflower florets, steamed
- Salt and black pepper to the taste
- ¼ teaspoon turmeric powder
- 1 and ½ teaspoons red chili powder
- 1 tablespoon ginger, grated
- 2 teaspoons lemon juice
- 3 tablespoons white flour
- 2 tablespoons water
- Cooking spray
- ½ teaspoon cornflour

Directions:
1. Mix chili powder with turmeric powder, ginger paste, salt, pepper, lemon juice, white flour, cornflour and water, stir, add cauliflower, toss well and transfer them to your Air Fryer's basket.
2. Coat them with cooking spray, cook them at 400°F for 10 minutes, divide them among plates and serve them as a side dish.
3. Enjoy!

Nutrition: calories 70, fat 1, fiber 2, carbs 12, protein 3

51. Fried Red Cabbage

Preparation time: 9 minutes **Cooking time:** 15 minutes **Servings:** 4
Ingredients:
- 4 garlic cloves, minced
- ½ cup yellow onion, chopped
- 1 tablespoon olive oil
- 6 cups red cabbage, chopped
- 1 cup veggie stock
- 1 tablespoon apple cider vinegar
- 1 cup applesauce
- Salt and black pepper to the taste

Directions:
1. In a heat-proof dish that fits your Air Fryer, mix cabbage with onion, garlic, oil, stock, vinegar, applesauce, salt and pepper, toss well, and place the dish in your Air Fryer's basket and cook at 380°F for 15 minutes.
2. Divide among plates and serve as a side dish.
3. Enjoy!

Nutrition: calories 172, fat 7, fiber 7, carbs 14, protein 5

52. Fried Tomatoes

Preparation time: 11 minutes **Cooking time:** 5 minutes **Servings:** 4
Ingredients:
- 2 green tomatoes, sliced
- Salt and black pepper to the taste
- ½ cup flour
- 1 cup buttermilk
- 1 cup panko breadcrumbs
- ½ tablespoon Creole seasoning
- Cooking spray

Directions:
1. Season tomato slices with salt and pepper.
2. Put flour in a bowl, buttermilk in another and panko crumbs and Creole seasoning in a third one. Dredge tomato slices in flour, then in buttermilk and panko bread crumb
3. Place them in your Air Fryer's basket greased with cooking spray and cook them at 400°F for 5 minutes.
4. Divide among plates and serve as a side dish.
5. Enjoy!

Nutrition: calories 124, fat 5, fiber 7, carbs 9, protein 3

53. Garlic Beet Wedges

Preparation time: 12 minutes **Cooking time:** 15 minutes **Servings:** 4
Ingredients:
- 4 beets, washed, peeled and cut into large wedges
- 1 tablespoon olive oil
- Salt and black to the taste
- 2 garlic cloves, minced
- 1 teaspoon lemon juice

Directions:
1. In a bowl, mix beets with oil, salt, pepper, garlic and lemon juice, toss well, transfer into your Air Fryer's basket and bake them at 400°F for 15 minutes.
2. Divide beets wedges among plates and serve as a side dish.
3. Enjoy!

Nutrition: calories 182, fat 6, fiber 3, carbs 8, protein 2

54. Greek Veggie Side Dish

Preparation time: 14 minutes **Cooking time:** 45 minutes **Servings:** 4
Ingredients:
- 1 eggplant, sliced
- 1 zucchini, sliced
- 2 red bell peppers, chopped
- 2 garlic cloves, minced
- 3 tablespoons olive oil
- 1 bay leaf
- 1 thyme spring, chopped
- 2 onions, chopped
- 4 tomatoes, cut into quarters
- Salt and black pepper to the taste

Directions:
1. In your Air Fryer's pan, mix eggplant slices with zucchini ones, bell peppers, garlic, oil, bay leaf, thyme, onions, tomatoes, salt and pepper, toss and cook them at 300°F for 35 minutes.
2. Divide among plates and serve as a side dish.
3. Enjoy!

Nutrition: calories 200, fat 1, fiber 3, carbs 7, protein 6

55. Green Beans Side Dish

Preparation time: 8 minutes **Cooking time:** 25 minutes **Servings:** 4
Ingredients:
- 1 and ½ pounds of green beans, trimmed and steamed for 2 minutes
- Salt and black pepper to the taste
- ½ pound shallots, chopped
- ¼ cup almonds, toasted
- 2 tablespoons olive oil

Directions:
1. In your Air Fryer's basket, mix green beans with salt, pepper, shallots, almonds and oil, toss well and cook at 400°F for 25 minutes.
2. Divide among plates and serve as a side dish.
3. Enjoy!

Nutrition: calories 152, fat 3, fiber 6, carbs 7, protein 4

56. Lemony Artichokes

Preparation time: 12 minutes **Cooking time:** 15 minutes **Servings:** 4
Ingredients:
- 2 medium artichokes, trimmed and halved
- Cooking spray
- 2 tablespoons lemon juice
- Salt and black pepper to the taste

Directions:
1. Grease your Air Fryer with cooking spray, add artichokes, drizzle lemon juice and sprinkle salt and black pepper and cook them at 380°F for 15 minutes.
2. Divide them into plates and serve as a side dish. Enjoy!

Nutrition: calories 121, fat 3, fiber 6, carbs 9, protein 4

57. Mushrooms and Sour Cream

Preparation time: 13 minutes **Cooking time:** 10 minutes **Servings:** 6
Ingredients:
- 2 bacon strips, chopped
- 1 yellow onion, chopped
- 1 green bell pepper, chopped
- 24 mushrooms, stems removed
- 1 carrot, grated
- ½ cup sour cream
- 1 cup cheddar cheese, grated
- Salt and black pepper to the taste

Directions:
1. Heat a pan over medium-high heat; add bacon, onion, bell pepper and carrot, stir and cook for 1 minute.
2. Add salt, pepper and sour cream, stir, cook for 1 minute more, take off the heat and cool down.
3. Stuff mushrooms with this mix, sprinkle cheese on top and cook at 360°F for 8 minutes.
4. Divide among plates and serve as a side dish.
5. Enjoy!

Nutrition: calories 211, fat 4, fiber 7, carbs 8, protein 3

58. Onion Rings Side Dish

Preparation time: 14 minutes **Cooking time:** 10 minutes **Servings:** 3
Ingredients:
- 1 onion cut into medium slices and rings separated

- 1 and ¼ cups white flour
- A pinch of salt
- 1 egg
- 1 cup of milk
- 1 teaspoon baking powder
- ¾ cup breadcrumbs

Directions:
1. Mix flour with salt and baking powder, stir, dredge onion rings in this mix and place them on a separate plate.
2. Add milk and egg to the flour mix and whisk well.
3. Dip onion rings in this mix, dredge them in breadcrumbs, put them in your Air Fryer's basket and cook them at 360°F for 10 minutes.
4. Divide among plates and serve as a side dish for a steak.
5. Enjoy!

Nutrition: cal. 140, fat 8, fiber 20, carbs 12, protein 3

59. Parmesan Mushrooms

Preparation time: 13 minutes **Cooking time:** 15 minutes **Servings:** 3

Ingredients:
- 9 button mushroom caps
- 3 cream cracker slices, crumbled
- 1 egg white
- 2 tablespoons parmesan, grated
- 1 teaspoon Italian seasoning
- A pinch of salt and black pepper
- 1 tablespoon butter, melted

Directions:
1. Mix crackers with egg white, parmesan, Italian seasoning, butter, salt and pepper, stir well and stuff mushrooms with this mix.
2. Arrange mushrooms in your Air Fryer's basket and cook them at 360°F for 15 minutes.
3. Divide among plates and serve as a side dish.
4. Enjoy!

Nutrition: calories 124, fat 4, fiber 4, carbs 7, protein 3

60. Potato Wedges

Preparation time: 14 minutes **Cooking time:** 25 minutes **Servings:** 4

Ingredients:
- 2 potatoes, cut into wedges
- 1 tablespoon olive oil
- Salt and black pepper to the taste
- 3 tablespoons sour cream
- 2 tablespoons sweet chili sauce

Directions:
1. Mix potato wedges with oil, salt and pepper, toss well, add to Air Fryer's basket and cook at 360°F for 25 minutes, flipping them once.
2. Divide potato wedges on plates, drizzle sour cream and chili sauce all over and serve them as a side dish.
3. Enjoy!

Nutrition: calories 171, fat 8, fiber 9, carbs 18, protein 7

61. Roasted Parsnips

Preparation time: 13 minutes **Cooking time:** 40 minutes **Servings:** 6

Ingredients:
- 2 pounds parsnips, peeled and cut into medium chunks
- 2 tablespoons maple syrup
- 1 tablespoon parsley flakes, dried
- 1 tablespoon olive oil

Directions:
1. Preheat your Air Fryer to 360°F, add oil and heat it.
2. Add parsnips, parsley flakes and maple syrup, toss and cook them for 40 minutes.
3. Divide among plates and serve as a side dish.
4. Enjoy!

Nutrition: calories 124, fat 3, fiber 3, carbs 7, protein 4

62. Roasted Peppers

Preparation time: 11 minutes **Cooking time:** 20 minutes **Servings:** 4

Ingredients:
- 1 tablespoon sweet paprika
- 1 tablespoon olive oil
- 4 red bell peppers, cut into medium strips
- 4 green bell peppers, cut into medium strips
- 4 yellow bell peppers, cut into medium strips
- 1 yellow onion, chopped
- Salt and black pepper to the taste

Directions:
1. Mix red bell peppers with green and yellow ones in your Air Fryer.
2. Add paprika, oil, onion, salt and pepper, toss and cook at 350°F for 20 minutes.
3. Divide among plates and serve as a side dish.
4. Enjoy!

Nutrition: calories 142, fat 4, fiber 4, carbs 7, protein 4

63. Roasted Pumpkin

Preparation time: 12 minutes **Cooking time:** 12 minutes **Servings:** 4
Ingredients:
- 1 and ½ pounds of pumpkin, deseeded, sliced, and roughly chopped
- 3 garlic cloves, minced
- 1 tablespoon olive oil
- A pinch of sea salt
- A pinch of brown sugar
- A pinch of nutmeg, ground
- A pinch of cinnamon powder

Directions:
1. In your Air Fryer's basket, mix pumpkin with garlic, oil, salt, brown sugar, cinnamon and nutmeg, toss well, cover and cook at 370°F for 12 minutes.
2. Divide among plates and serve.
3. Enjoy!

Nutrition: calories 200, fat 5, fiber 4, carbs 7, protein 4

64. Sweet Potato Fries

Preparation time: 14 minutes **Cooking time:** 20 minutes **Servings:** 2
Ingredients:
- 2 sweet potatoes, peeled and cut into medium fries
- Salt and black pepper to the taste
- 2 tablespoons olive oil
- ½ teaspoon curry powder
- ¼ teaspoon coriander, ground
- ¼ cup ketchup
- 2 tablespoons mayonnaise
- ½ teaspoon cumin, ground
- A pinch of ginger powder
- A pinch of cinnamon powder

Directions:
1. In your Air Fryer's basket, mix sweet potato fries with salt, pepper, coriander, curry powder and oil, toss well and cook at 370°F for 20 minutes, flipping them once.
2. Meanwhile, mix ketchup with mayo, cumin, ginger and cinnamon in a bowl and whisk well.
3. Divide fries among plates, drizzle ketchup mix over them and serve as a side dish.
4. Enjoy!

Nutrition: calories 200, fat 5, fiber 8, carbs 9, protein 7

65. Veggie Fries

Preparation time: 11 minutes **Cooking time:** 30 minutes **Servings:** 4
Ingredients:
- 4 parsnips, cut into medium sticks
- 2 sweet potatoes cut into medium sticks
- 4 mixed carrots cut into medium sticks
- Salt and black pepper to the taste
- 2 tablespoons rosemary, chopped
- 2 tablespoons olive oil
- 1 tablespoon flour
- ½ teaspoon garlic powder

Directions:
1. Put veggie fries in a bowl, add oil, garlic powder, salt, pepper, flour and rosemary and toss to coat.
2. Put sweet potatoes in your preheated Air Fryer, cook them for 10 minutes at 350°F and transfer them to a platter.
3. Put parsnip fries in your Air Fryer, cook for 5 minutes and transfer over potato fries.
4. Put carrot fries in your Air Fryer, cook for 15 minutes at 350°F and transfer to the platter with the other fries.
5. Divide veggie fries among plates and serve them as a side dish.
6. Enjoy!

Nutrition: calories 100, fat 0, fiber 4, carbs 7, protein 4

66. Zucchini Croquettes

Preparation time: 12 minutes **Cooking time:** 10 minutes **Servings:** 4
Ingredients:
- 1 carrot, grated
- 1 zucchini, grated
- 2 slices of bread crumbled
- 1 egg
- Salt and black pepper to the taste
- ½ teaspoon sweet paprika
- 1 teaspoon garlic, minced
- 2 tablespoons parmesan cheese, grated
- 1 tablespoon of cornflour

Directions:
1. Put zucchini in a bowl, add salt, leave aside for 10 minutes, squeeze excess water and transfer them to another bowl.
2. Add carrots, salt, pepper, paprika, garlic, flour, parmesan, egg, and breadcrumbs, stir well, shape 8 croquettes, place them in your Air Fryer and cook at 360°F for 10 minutes.
3. Divide among plates and serve as a side dish
4. Enjoy!

Nutrition: calories 100, fat 3, fiber 1, carbs 7, protein 4

67. Zucchini Fries

Preparation time: 13 minutes **Cooking time:** 12 minutes **Servings:** 4
Ingredients:
- 1 zucchini, cut into medium sticks
- A drizzle of olive oil
- Salt and black pepper to the taste
- 2 eggs, whisked
- 1 cup breadcrumbs
- ½ cup flour

Directions:
1. Put flour in a bowl, mix with salt and pepper, and stir.
2. Put breadcrumbs in another bowl.
3. Mix eggs with salt and pepper in a third bowl.
4. Place the zucchini fries in the flour, then in the eggs and breadcrumbs at the end.
5. Grease your Air Fryer with some olive oil, heat up at 400°F, add zucchini fries and cook them for 12 minutes.
6. Serve them as a side dish. Enjoy!

Nutrition: calories 172, fat 3, fiber 3, carbs 7, protein 3

SNACKS & APPETIZERS

68. Apple Chips

Preparation time: 13 minutes **Cooking time:** 10 minutes **Servings:** 2
Ingredients:
- 1 apple, cored and sliced
- A pinch of salt
- ½ teaspoon cinnamon powder
- 1 tablespoon white sugar

Directions:
1. Mix apple slices, salt, sugar and cinnamon in a bowl, toss, transfer to your fryer basket and cook for 10 minutes at 390 °F, turning once.
2. Arrange crisps in bowls and serve. Enjoy!

Nutrition: calories 71, fat 0, fiber 4, carbs 3, protein 1

69. Banana Snack

Preparation time: 12 minutes **Cooking time:** 5 minutes **Servings:** 8
Ingredients:
- 16 cups of pastry
- ¼ cup of peanut butter
- ¾ cup of chocolate chips
- 1 banana, peeled and chopped into 16 pieces
- 1 tablespoon vegetable oil

Directions:
1. Place the chocolate chips in a small pan, heat over low heat, stir until it melts and remove the heat.
2. Add the peanut butter to the coconut oil and whisk well in a bowl. Pour 1 tsp of chocolate mixture into a cup, add 1 slice of banana and top with 1 tsp of butter.
3. Repeat with the remaining cups, place them all in a dish suitable for your fryer and bake at 320°F for 5 minutes. Put them in the freezer and keep them until you give them a snack. Enjoy!

Nutrition: calories 71, fat 4, fiber 1, carbs 10, protein 1

70. Beef Jerky Snack

Preparation time: 2 hours **Cooking time:** 1 hour and 30 minutes **Servings:** 6
Ingredients:
- 2 cups soy sauce
- ½ cup Worcestershire sauce
- 2 tablespoons black peppercorns
- 2 tablespoons black pepper
- 2 pounds of beef round, sliced

Directions:
1. Combine soy sauce with black pepper, black pepper and Worcestershire sauce in a bowl and beat well.
2. Add slices of beef, mix to coat and refrigerate for 6 hours. Put the beef balls in your fryer and cook them at 370°F for 1 hour and 30 minutes.
3. Transfer into a bowl and serve chilled. Enjoy!

Nutrition: calories 302, fat 12, fiber 4, carbs 3, protein 8

71. Bread Sticks

Preparation time: 13 minutes **Cooking time:** 11 minutes **Servings:** 2
Ingredients:
- 4 slices of bread, each cut into 4 strips
- 2 eggs
- ¼ cup of milk
- 1 teaspoon of cinnamon powder
- 1 tablespoon of honey

- ¼ cup of brown sugar
- A pinch of nutmeg

Directions:
1. Combine eggs with milk, brown sugar, cinnamon, nutmeg and honey in a bowl and whisk thoroughly.
2. Dip the breadsticks in this mixture, place them in your Air Fryer cart and cook at 360°F for 10 minutes.
3. Arrange breadsticks in bowls and serve. Enjoy!

Nutrition: calories 141, fat 1, fiber 4, carbs 8, protein 4

72. Calamari and Shrimp Snack

Preparation time: 16 minutes **Cooking time:** 20 minutes **Servings:** 1
Ingredients:
- 8 ounces calamari, cut into medium rings
- 7 ounces shrimp, peeled and deveined
- 1 egg
- 3 tablespoons white flour
- 1 tablespoon olive oil
- 2 tablespoons avocado, chopped
- 1 teaspoon tomato paste
- 1 tablespoon mayonnaise
- A splash of Worcestershire sauce
- 1 teaspoon of lemon juice
- Salt and black pepper to the taste
- ½ teaspoon turmeric powder

Directions:
1. In a bowl, beat the egg with oil, add the calamari rings and shrimp and coat well.
2. Mix flour with salt, pepper and turmeric in another bowl and stir.
3. Dredge calamari and shrimp in the mix, place them in your Air Fryer's basket and bake at 350°F for 9 minutes, flipping them once.
4. Meanwhile, mix avocado with mayo and tomato paste in a bowl and mash using a fork.
5. Add Worcestershire sauce, lemon juice, salt and pepper and stir well.
6. Arrange calamari and shrimp on a platter and serve with the sauce on the side. Enjoy!

Nutrition: cal 288, fat 23, fiber 3, carbs 10, protein 15

73. Cauliflower Bars

Preparation time: 12 minutes **Cooking time:** 25 minutes **Servings:** 12
Ingredients:
- 1 big cauliflower head, florets separated
- ½ cup mozzarella, shredded
- ¼ cup egg whites

- 1 teaspoon Italian seasoning
- Salt and black pepper to the taste

Directions:
1. Put the cauliflower florets in your food processor, pulse them, and place them on a lined baking sheet suitable for your air fryer.
2. Introduce them to the air fryer and bake them at 360°F for 10 minutes.
3. Transfer the cauliflower to a bowl, add salt, pepper, the cheese, egg whites and Italian seasoning and toss to combine.
4. Spread it in a rectangular pan that fits your fryer, press well, place it in the fryer and cook at 360°F for another 15 minutes.
5. Slice into 12 bars, put on a tray and serve. Enjoy!

Nutrition: calories 53, fat 1, fiber 2, carbs 3, protein 3

74. Cheese Sticks

Preparation time: 1 hour and 13 minutes **Cooking time:** 8 minutes **Servings:** 16
Ingredients:
- 2 eggs, whisked
- Salt and black pepper to the taste
- 8 mozzarella cheese strings, cut into halves
- 1 cup parmesan, grated
- 1 tablespoon Italian seasoning
- Cooking spray
- 1 garlic clove, minced

Directions:
1. Mix parmesan with salt, pepper, Italian seasoning and garlic in a bowl and stir well.
2. Put whisked eggs in another bowl.
3. Dip mozzarella sticks in the egg mixture, then in the cheese mix.
4. Dip them in egg and parmesan mix and keep them in the freezer for 1 hour.
5. Spray cheese sticks with cooking oil, place them in the Air Fryer's basket and cook at 390°F for 8 minutes, flipping them halfway.
6. Arrange them on a platter and serve. Enjoy!

Nutrition: calories 140, fat 5, fiber 1, carbs 3, protein 4

75. Coconut Chicken Bites

Preparation time: 11 minutes **Cooking time:** 13 minutes **Servings:** 4
Ingredients:
- 2 teaspoons garlic powder
- 2 eggs
- Salt and black pepper to the taste

- ¾ cup panko breadcrumbs
- ¾ cup coconut, shredded
- Cooking spray
- 8 chicken tenders

Directions:
1. Combine eggs, salt, pepper, and garlic powder in a bowl and whisk well.
2. Mix coconut with panko in another bowl and stir well.
3. Soak the chicken tenderloins in the egg mixture, then coat them with the coconut. Coat the chicken bites with cooking spray, place in your fryer basket and bake them at 350°F for 10 minutes.
4. Place them on a platter and serve. Enjoy!

Nutrition: calories 253, fat 4, fiber 2, carbs 14, protein 24

76. Crab Sticks

Preparation time: 14 minutes **Cooking time:** 12 minutes **Servings:** 4
Ingredients:
- 10 crabsticks, halved
- 2 teaspoons sesame oil
- 2 teaspoons Cajun seasoning

Directions:
1. Put the crab sticks in a bowl, add the sesame oil and Cajun seasoning, toss, transfer to the basket of your fryer and cook at 350°F for 12 minutes.
2. Arrange on a platter and serve. Enjoy!

Nutrition: calories 111, fat 0, fiber 1, carbs 4, protein 2

77. Crispy Fish Sticks

Preparation time: 12 minutes **Cooking time:** 12 minutes **Servings:** 2
Ingredients:
- 4 ounces of breadcrumbs
- 4 tbsp olive oil
- 1 egg, beaten
- 4 white fish filets, boneless, skinless and cut into medium sticks
- Salt and black pepper to the taste

Directions:
1. In a bowl, combine the breadcrumbs with the oil and stir. Place the egg in another bowl, season with salt and pepper and whisk well.
2. Dip the fish stick in the egg and then in the breadcrumb mix, place it in your air fryer basket and cook at 360°F for 12 minutes.
3. Place the fish sticks on a tray and serve. Enjoy!

Nutrition: calories 161, fat 3, fiber 5, carbs 12, protein 3

78. Empanadas

Preparation time: 13 minutes **Cooking time:** 25 minutes **Servings:** 4
Ingredients:
- 1 package of empanada shells
- 1 tablespoon olive oil
- 1 pound of beef meat, ground
- 1 yellow onion, chopped
- Salt and black pepper to the taste
- 2 garlic cloves, minced
- ½ teaspoon cumin, ground
- ¼ cup tomato salsa
- 1 egg yolk whisked with 1 tablespoon of water
- 1 green bell pepper, chopped

Directions:
1. Heat skillet with oil over medium-high heat; add beef and fry on all sides. Add the onion, garlic, salt, pepper, pepper and tomato sauce, toss and cook for 15 minutes.
2. Divide the cooked meat among the empanadas, brush with the egg and seal. Put them in your Air Fryer steamer basket and cook in 350°F for 10 minutes.
3. Arrange in a tray and serve. Enjoy!

Nutrition: cal 275, fat 17, fiber 14, carbs 20, protein 7

79. Fish Nuggets

Preparation time: 14 minutes **Cooking time:** 12 minutes **Servings:** 4
Ingredients:
- 28 ounces of fish fillets, skinless and cut into medium pieces
- salt and black pepper to the taste
- 5 tablespoons flour
- 1 egg, whisked

- 5 tablespoons water
- 3 ounces panko breadcrumbs
- 1 tablespoon garlic powder
- 1 tablespoon smoked paprika
- 4 tablespoons homemade mayonnaise
- Lemon juice from ½ lemon
- 1 teaspoon dill, dried
- Cooking spray

Directions:
1. In a bowl, combine the flour and water and toss to combine. Add the egg, salt and pepper and whisk to combine.
2. Mix panko with garlic powder and paprika in a second bowl and toss to combine. Dip the fish pieces into the flour and egg mixture, then into the panko mixture.
3. Put them in your fryer basket, spray them with cooking oil and cook at 400°F for 12 minutes. In the meantime, mix the mayonnaise with the dill and lemon juice in a bowl and whisk well.
4. Arrange the fish chips on a plate and serve with the dill mayonnaise. Enjoy!

Nutrition: cal 333, fat 12, fiber 6, carbs 17, protein 15

80. Greek Lamb Meatballs

Preparation time: 14 minutes **Cooking time:** 8 minutes **Servings:** 10
Ingredients:
- 4 ounces of lamb meat, minced
- Salt and black pepper to the taste
- 1 slice of bread, toasted and crumbled
- 2 tablespoons feta cheese, crumbled
- ½ tablespoon lemon peel, grated
- 1 tablespoon oregano, chopped

Directions:
In a bowl, combine the meat with the breadcrumbs, salt, pepper, feta, oregano and lemon rind.
Bake at 400°F for 8 minutes, place on a tray and serve. Enjoy!

Nutrition: cal 235, fat 12, fiber 2, carbs 20, protein 30

81. Roasted Bell Pepper Rolls

Preparation time: 9 minutes **Cooking time:** 10 minutes **Servings:** 8
Ingredients:
- 1 yellow bell pepper, halved
- 1 orange bell pepper, halved
- Salt and black pepper to the taste
- 4 ounces feta cheese, crumbled
- 1 green onion, chopped
- 2 tablespoons oregano, chopped

Directions:
1. Mix cheese with onion, oregano, salt and pepper in a bowl and whisk well.
2. Place bell pepper halves in your Air Fryer's basket, cook at 400°F for 10 minutes, transfer to a cutting board, cool down and peel.
3. Divide cheese mix on each bell pepper in half, roll, secure with toothpicks, arrange on a platter and serve as an appetizer. Enjoy!

Nutrition: calories 170, fat 1, fiber 2, carbs 8, protein 5

82. Salmon Meatballs

Preparation time: 14 minutes **Cooking time:** 12 minutes **Servings:** 4
Ingredients:
- 3 tablespoons cilantro, minced
- 1 pound salmon, skinless and chopped
- 1 small yellow onion, chopped
- 1 egg white
- Salt and black pepper to the taste
- 2 garlic cloves, minced
- ½ teaspoon paprika
- ¼ cup panko
- ½ teaspoon oregano, ground
- Cooking spray

Directions:
1. Mix the salmon with the onion, coriander, the egg white, garlic cloves, salt and pepper, paprika and oregano in your robot and stir well.
2. Add the panko, stir again and shape the meatballs out of this mixture using your palms.
3. Put them in your fryer basket, spray them with cooking spray and cook at 320°F for 12 minutes, shaking the fryer halfway. Lay the meatballs on a platter and serve as a starter. Enjoy!

Nutrition: cal 290, fat 12, fiber 3, carbs 22, protein 23

83. Salmon Party Patties

Preparation time: 13 minutes **Cooking time:** 22 minutes **Servings:** 4
Ingredients:
- 3 big potatoes, boiled, drained and mashed
- 1 big salmon fillet, skinless, boneless
- 2 tablespoons parsley, chopped
- 2 tablespoon dills, chopped
- Salt and black pepper to the taste
- 1 egg
- 2 tablespoons breadcrumbs

- Cooking spray

Directions:
1. Put the salmon in your Air Fryer cart and cook for 10 minutes at 360°F. Transfer the salmon onto a chopping board, cool it, crumble it and place it in a bowl.
2. Combine puree, salt, pepper, dill, parsley, egg, and breadcrumbs. Place the salmon patties in your frying pan and spray them with cooking oil.
3. Bake at 360°F for 12 minutes, turning halfway, transfer to a serving platter and serve. Enjoy!

Nutrition: calories 231, fat 3, fiber 7, carbs 14, protein 4

84. Seafood Appetizer

Preparation time: 16 minutes **Cooking time:** 25 minutes **Servings:** 4
Ingredients:
- ½ cup yellow onion, chopped
- 1 cup green bell pepper, chopped
- 1 cup celery, chopped
- 1 cup baby shrimp, peeled and deveined
- 1 cup crabmeat, flaked
- 1 cup homemade mayonnaise
- 1 teaspoon Worcestershire sauce
- Salt and black pepper to the taste
- 2 tablespoons breadcrumbs
- 1 tablespoon butter
- 1 teaspoon sweet paprika

Directions:
1. Toss shrimp with crab meat, bell pepper, onion, mayonnaise, celery, salt and pepper. Add the Worcestershire sauce, stir again and pour it all into a baking dish suitable for your fryer.
2. Sprinkle with breadcrumbs and add butter; place in the air fryer and cook at 320°F for 25 minutes, stirring halfway.
3. Arrange in bowls and serve with paprika sprinkled over the top as a starter. Enjoy!

Nutrition: calories 200, fat 1, fiber 2, carbs 5, protein 1

85. Shrimp and Chestnut Rolls

Preparation time: 12 minutes **Cooking time:** 15 minutes **Servings:** 4
Ingredients:
- ½ pound already cooked shrimp, chopped
- 8 ounces of water chestnuts, chopped
- ½ pounds of shiitake mushrooms, chopped
- 2 cups cabbage, chopped
- 2 tablespoons olive oil
- 1 garlic clove, minced
- 1 teaspoon ginger, grated
- 3 scallions, chopped
- Salt and black pepper to the taste
- 1 tablespoon water
- 1 egg yolk
- 6 spring roll wrappers

Directions:
1. Heat a pan with the oil over medium-high heat; add cabbage, shrimp, chestnuts, mushrooms, garlic, ginger, scallions, salt and pepper, stir and cook for 2 minutes.
2. In a bowl, mix egg with water and stir well.
3. Arrange roll wrappers on a working surface, divide shrimp and veggie mix on them, seal edges with egg wash, place them all in your Air Fryer's basket, cook at 360°F for 15 minutes.
4. Transfer to a platter and serve. Enjoy!

Nutrition: calories 140, fat 3, fiber 1, carbs 12, protein 3

86. Stuffed Peppers

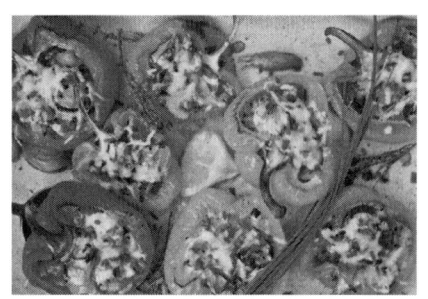

Preparation time: 10 minutes **Cooking time:** 8 minutes **Servings:** 8
Ingredients:
- 8 small bell peppers, tops cut off and seeds removed
- 1 tablespoon olive oil
- Salt and black pepper to the taste
- 3.5 ounces goat cheese, cut into 8 pieces

Directions:
1. Mix cheese with oil, salt and pepper and toss to coat.
2. Stuff each pepper with goat cheese, place them in the Air Fryer basket, bake at 400°F for 8 minutes, arrange on a platter and serve. Enjoy!

Nutrition: calories 120, fat 1, fiber 1, carbs 12, protein 8

87. Sweet Bacon Snack

Preparation time: 11 minutes **Cooking time:** 30 minutes **Servings:** 16
Ingredients:
- ½ teaspoon cinnamon powder
- 16 bacon slices
- 1 tablespoon avocado oil

- 3 ounces dark chocolate
- 1 teaspoon maple extract

Directions:
1. Arrange bacon slices in your Air Fryer's basket, sprinkle cinnamon mix over them and cook them at 300°F for 30 minutes.
2. Heat a pot with the oil over medium heat, add chocolate and stir until it melts.
3. Add maple extract, stir, take off the heat and leave aside to cool down a bit.
4. Take bacon strips out of the oven, leave them to cool down, dip each in chocolate mix, place them on parchment paper and cool down completely. Serve cold as a snack. Enjoy!

Nutrition: calories 200, fat 4, fiber 5, carbs 12, protein 3

88. Sweet Popcorn

Preparation time: 7 minutes **Cooking time:** 10 minutes
Servings: 4
Ingredients:
- 2 tablespoons corn kernels
- 2 and ½ tablespoons of butter
- 2 ounces brown sugar

Directions:
1. Put corn kernels in your Air Fryer's pan, cook at 400°F for 6 minutes, transfer them to a tray, spread and leave aside for now.
2. Heat a pan over low heat, add butter, melt it, add sugar and stir until it dissolves.
3. Add popcorn, toss to coat, take off the heat and spread on the tray again.
4. Cooldown, divide into bowls and serve as a snack. Enjoy!

Nutrition: calories 70, fat 0.2, fiber 0, carbs 1, protein 1

89. Zucchini Chips

Preparation time: 13 minutes **Cooking time:** 1-hour
Servings: 6
Ingredients:
- 3 zucchinis, thinly sliced
- Salt and black pepper to the taste
- 2 tablespoons olive oil
- 2 tablespoons balsamic vinegar

Directions:
1. Mix oil with vinegar, salt and pepper and whisk well.
2. Add zucchini slices, toss to coat well, introduce in your Air Fryer and cook at 200°F for 1 hour.
3. Serve zucchini chips cold as a snack. Enjoy!

Nutrition: calories 40, fat 3, fiber 7, carbs 3, protein 3.

FISH & SEAFOOD

90. Air Fried Branzino

Preparation time: 12 minutes **Cooking time:** 10 minutes **Servings:** 4
Ingredients:
- Zest from 1 lemon, grated
- Zest from 1 orange, grated
- Juice from ½ lemon
- Juice from ½ orange
- Salt and black pepper to the taste
- 4 medium branzino fillets, boneless
- ½ cup parsley, chopped
- 2 tablespoons olive oil
- A pinch of red pepper flakes, crushed

Directions:
1. In a large bowl, mix fish fillets with lemon zest, orange zest, lemon juice, orange juice, salt, pepper, oil and pepper flakes, toss well, and transfer fillets to your preheated Air Fryer at 350°F and bake for 10 minutes, flipping fillets once.
2. Divide fish on plates, sprinkle with parsley and serve right away. Enjoy!

Nutrition: cal 260, fat 8, fiber 12, carbs 21, protein 12

91. Air Fried Cod

Preparation time: 12 minutes **Cooking time:** 12 minutes **Servings:** 4
Ingredients:
- 2 codfish, 7 ounces each
- A drizzle of sesame oil
- Salt and black pepper to the taste
- 1 cup water
- 1 teaspoon dark soy sauce
- 4 tablespoons light soy sauce
- 1 tablespoon sugar
- 3 tablespoons olive oil
- 4 ginger slices
- 3 spring onions, chopped
- 2 tablespoons coriander, chopped

Directions:
1. Season the fish with salt and pepper, sprinkle with sesame oil, rub well and let rest for 10 minutes.
2. Add the fish to your skillet and cook at 356°F for 12 minutes. Meanwhile, heat a skillet with the water over medium heat; add the dark, light soy sauce and sugar, stir, bring to a boil and remove the heat.
3. Heat a frying pan with olive oil over medium heat; add ginger and scallions, stir, cook for a few minutes and remove from heat.
4. Place the fish on the plates, top with ginger and green onions, pour in the soy sauce mixture, sprinkle with coriander and serve immediately.

Nutrition: cal 301, fat 17, fiber 8, carbs 20, protein 22

92. Asian Halibut

Preparation time: 32 minutes **Cooking time:** 10 minutes **Servings:** 3
Ingredients:
- 1 pound halibut steaks
- 2/3 cup soy sauce
- ¼ cup sugar
- 2 tablespoons lime juice
- ½ cup mirin
- ¼ teaspoon red pepper flakes, crushed
- ¼ cup orange juice
- ¼ teaspoon ginger, grated
- 1 garlic clove, minced

Directions:
1. Add the soy sauce to a skillet, heat over medium heat and add the mirin, sugar, lime and orange juice, pepper flakes, ginger and garlic.
2. Blend well, bring to a boil and remove from the heat. Transfer half the marinade into a bowl, add

the halibut, coat thoroughly and refrigerate for 30 minutes.
3. Transfer halibut to your Air Fryer and bake at 390°F for 10 minutes, flipping once.
4. Spread the halibut steaks on the plates, drizzle the rest of the marinade and serve hot. Enjoy!

Nutrition: cal 286, fat 5, fiber 12, carbs 14, protein 23

93. Creamy Shrimp and Veggies

Preparation time: 10 minutes **Cooking time:** 30 minutes **Servings:** 4
Ingredients:
- 8 ounces mushrooms, chopped
- 1 asparagus bunch, cut into medium pieces
- 1 pound shrimp, peeled and deveined
- Salt and black pepper to the taste
- 1 spaghetti squash, cut into halves
- 2 tablespoons olive oil
- 2 teaspoons Italian seasoning
- 1 yellow onion, chopped
- 1 teaspoon red pepper flakes, crushed
- ¼ cup butter, melted
- 1 cup parmesan cheese, grated
- 2 garlic cloves, minced
- 1 cup heavy cream

Directions:
1. Place squash halves in your Air Fryer's basket, cook at 390°F for 17 minutes, transfer to a cutting board, scoop insides and transfer to a bowl.
2. Put water in a pot, add some salt, bring to a boil, add asparagus, steam for a couple of minutes, transfer to a bowl full of ice water, drain and leave aside as well.
3. Heat a pan that fits your Air Fryer with the oil over medium heat, add onions and mushrooms, stir and cook for 7 minutes.
4. Add pepper flakes, Italian seasoning, salt, squash, asparagus, shrimp, melted butter, cream, parmesan and garlic, toss and cook in your Air Fryer at 360°F for 6 minutes.
5. Divide everything into plates and serve. Enjoy!

Nutrition: calories 325, fat 6, fiber 5, carbs 14, protein 13

94. Crusted Salmon

Preparation time: 12 minutes **Cooking time:** 10 minutes **Servings:** 4
Ingredients:
- 1 cup pistachios, chopped
- 4 salmon fillets
- ¼ cup lemon juice
- 2 tablespoons honey
- 1 teaspoon dill, chopped
- Salt and black pepper to the taste
- 1 tablespoon mustard

Directions:
1. Mix pistachios with mustard, honey, lemon juice, salt, black pepper and dill, whisk and spread over salmon.
2. Put in your Air Fryer and cook at 350°F for 10 minutes.
3. Divide among plates and serve with a side salad.
4. Enjoy!

Nutrition: cal 300, fat 17, fiber 12, carbs 20, protein 22

95. Delicious Catfish

Preparation time: 12 minutes **Cooking time:** 20 minutes **Servings:** 4
Ingredients:
- 4 catfish fillets
- Salt and black pepper to the taste
- A pinch of sweet paprika
- 1 tablespoon parsley, chopped
- 1 tablespoon lemon juice
- 1 tablespoon olive oil

Directions:
1. Season catfish fillets with salt, pepper and paprika, drizzle oil, rub well, place in your Air Fryer's basket and cook at 400°F for 20 minutes, flipping the fish after 10 minutes.
2. Divide fish on plates, drizzle lemon juice, sprinkle parsley and serve. Enjoy!

Nutrition: cal 253, fat 6, fiber 12, carbs 26, protein 22

96. Delicious Red Snapper

Preparation time: 32 minutes **Cooking time:** 15 minutes **Servings:** 4
Ingredients:
- 1 big red snapper, cleaned and scored
- Salt and black pepper to the taste
- 3 garlic cloves, minced
- 1 jalapeno, chopped
- ¼ pound okra, chopped
- 1 tablespoon butter
- 2 tablespoons olive oil
- 1 red bell pepper, chopped
- 2 tablespoons white wine
- 2 tablespoons parsley, chopped

Directions:
1. Mix jalapeno, and wine with garlic, stir well and rub snapper with this mix.

2. Season fish with salt and pepper and leave it aside for 30 minutes.
3. Meanwhile, heat a pan with 1 tablespoon butter over medium heat, add bell pepper and okra, stir and cook for 5 minutes.
4. Stuff the red snapper's belly with this mix, add parsley and rub with the olive oil.
5. Place in preheated Air Fryer and cook at 400°F for 15 minutes, flipping the fish halfway.
6. Divide among plates and serve. Enjoy!

Nutrition: calori. 261, fat 7, fiber 18, carbs 28, protein 18

97. Fish and Couscous

Preparation time: 11 minutes **Cooking time:** 15 minutes **Servings:** 4
Ingredients:
- 2 red onions, chopped
- Cooking spray
- 2 small fennel bulbs, cored and sliced
- ¼ cup almonds, toasted and sliced
- Salt and black pepper to the taste
- 2 and ½ pounds of sea bass, gutted
- 5 teaspoons fennel seeds
- ¾ cup whole wheat couscous, cooked

Directions:
1. Season fish with salt and pepper, spray with cooking spray, place in your Air Fryer and cook at 350°F for 10 minutes.
2. Meanwhile, spray a pan with cooking oil and heat it over medium heat.
3. Add fennel seeds to this pan, stir and toast them for 1 minute.
4. Add onion, salt, pepper, fennel bulbs, almonds and couscous, stir, cook for 2-3 minutes and divide among plates.
5. Add fish next to the couscous mix and serve right away. Enjoy!

Nutrition: cal. 354, fat 7, fiber 10, carbs 20, protein 30

98. Honey Sea Bass

Preparation time: 11 minutes **Cooking time:** 10 minutes **Servings:** 2
Ingredients:
- 2 sea bass fillets
- Zest from ½ orange, grated
- Juice from ½ orange
- A pinch of salt and black pepper
- 2 tablespoons mustard
- 2 teaspoons honey
- 2 tablespoons olive oil
- ½ pound canned lentils, drained
- A small bunch of dill, chopped
- 2 ounces watercress
- A small bunch of parsley, chopped

Directions:
1. Season fish fillets with salt and pepper, add orange zest and juice, rub with 1 tablespoon oil, honey and mustard, rub, transfer to your Air Fryer and bake at 350°F for 10 minutes, flipping halfway.
2. Meanwhile, put lentils in a small pot, warm it up over medium heat, add the rest of the oil, watercress, dill and parsley, stir well and divide among plates.
3. Add fish fillets and serve right away. Enjoy!

Nutrition: calories 212, fat 8, fiber 12, carbs 9, protein 17

99. Italian Barramundi Fillets and Tomato Salsa

Preparation time: 10 minutes **Cooking time:** 8 minutes **Servings:** 4
Ingredients:
- 2 barramundi fillets, boneless
- 1 tablespoon olive oil+ 2 teaspoons
- 2 teaspoons Italian seasoning
- ¼ cup green olives, pitted and chopped
- ¼ cup cherry tomatoes, chopped
- ¼ cup black olives, chopped
- 1 tablespoon lemon zest
- 2 tablespoons lemon zest
- Salt and black pepper to the taste
- 2 tablespoons parsley, chopped

Directions:
1. Rub fish with salt, pepper, Italian seasoning and 2 teaspoons olive oil, transfer to your Air Fryer and cook at 360°F for 8 minutes, flipping them halfway.
2. Mix tomatoes with black olives, green olives, salt, pepper, lemon zest, lemon juice, parsley and 1 tablespoon olive oil and toss well.
3. Divide fish on plates, add tomato salsa on top and serve. Enjoy!

Nutrition: calories 270, fat 4, fiber 2, carbs 18, protein 27

100. Lemon Sole and Swiss Chard

Preparation time: 10 minutes **Cooking time:** 14 minutes **Servings:** 4
Ingredients:
- 1 teaspoon lemon zest, grated
- 4 white bread slices, quartered
- ¼ cup walnuts, chopped
- ¼ cup parmesan, grated
- 4 tablespoons olive oil
- 4 sole fillets, boneless
- Salt and black pepper to the taste
- 4 tablespoons butter
- ¼ cup lemon juice
- 3 tablespoons capers
- 2 garlic cloves, minced
- 2 bunches of Swiss chard, chopped

Directions:
1. Mix bread with walnuts, cheese and lemon zest in your food processor and pulse well.
2. Add half of the olive oil, pulse well again and leave aside for now.
3. Heat a pan with the butter over medium heat; add lemon juice, salt, pepper and capers, stir well, add fish and toss it.
4. Transfer the fish to your preheated Air Fryer's basket, top it with the bread mix you've made at the beginning and bake at 350°F for 14 minutes.
5. Meanwhile, heat another pan with the rest of the oil, add garlic, Swiss chard, salt and pepper, stir gently, cook for 2 minutes and take off the heat.
6. Divide fish among plates and serve with sautéed chard on the side. Enjoy!

Nutrition: cal 321, fat 7, fiber 18, carbs 27, protein 12

101. Lemony Saba Fish

Preparation time: 10 minutes **Cooking time:** 8 minutes **Servings:** 1
Ingredients:
- 4 Saba fish fillet, boneless
- Salt and black pepper to the taste
- 3 red chili peppers, chopped
- 2 tablespoons lemon juice
- 2 tablespoon olive oil
- 2 tablespoon garlic, minced

Directions:
1. Sprinkle the fish fillets with salt and pepper and put them in a bowl.
2. Add lemon juice, oil, chili and garlic and toss to coat; transfer fish to your Air Fryer and cook at 360°F for 8 minutes, flipping halfway.
3. Divide among plates and serve with some fries.

Nutrition: calories 300, fat 4, fiber 8, carbs 15, protein 15

102. Marinated Salmon

Preparation time: 1-hour **Cooking time:** 20 minutes **Servings:** 6
Ingredients:
- 1 whole salmon
- 1 tablespoon dill, chopped
- 1 tablespoon tarragon, chopped
- 1 tablespoon garlic, minced
- Juice from 2 lemons
- 1 lemon, sliced
- A pinch of salt and black pepper

Directions:
1. Mix fish with salt, pepper and lemon juice, toss well and keep in the fridge for 1 hour. Stuff salmon with garlic and lemon slices, place in your Air Fryer's basket and cook at 320°F for 25 minutes.
2. Divide among plates and serve with a tasty coleslaw on the side. Enjoy!

Nutrition: calories 300, fat 8, fiber 9, carbs 19, protein 27

103. Salmon and Avocado Salad

Preparation time: 14 minutes **Cooking time:** 20 minutes **Servings:** 4
Ingredients:
- 2 medium salmon fillets
- ¼ cup melted butter
- 4 ounces mushrooms, sliced
- Sea salt and black pepper to the taste
- 12 cherry tomatoes, halved
- 2 tablespoons olive oil
- 8 ounces of lettuce leaves, torn
- 1 avocado, pitted, peeled and cubed
- 1 jalapeno pepper, chopped
- 5 cilantro springs, chopped
- 2 tablespoons white wine vinegar
- 1-ounce feta cheese, crumbled

Directions:
1. Place salmon on a lined baking sheet, brush with 2 tablespoons melted butter, season with salt and pepper, boil for 15 minutes over medium heat and then keep warm.
2. Meanwhile, heat a pan with the rest of the butter over medium heat, add mushrooms, stir and cook for a few minutes.
3. Put tomatoes in a bowl, add salt, pepper and 1 tablespoon of olive oil and toss to coat.

4. Mix salmon with mushrooms, lettuce, avocado, tomatoes, jalapeno and cilantro.
5. Add the rest of the oil, vinegar, salt and pepper, sprinkle cheese on top and serve. Enjoy!

Nutrition: calories 235, fat 6, fiber 8, carbs 19, protein 5

104. Shrimp and Crab Mix

Preparation time: 13 minutes **Cooking time:** 25 minutes **Servings:** 4
Ingredients:
- ½ cup yellow onion, chopped
- 1 cup green bell pepper, chopped
- 1 cup celery, chopped
- 1 pound shrimp, peeled and deveined
- 1 cup crabmeat, flaked
- 1 cup mayonnaise
- 1 teaspoon Worcestershire sauce
- Salt and black pepper to the taste
- 2 tablespoons breadcrumbs
- 1 tablespoon butter, melted
- 1 teaspoon sweet paprika

Directions:
1. In a bowl, mix shrimp with crab meat, bell pepper, onion, mayo, celery, salt, pepper and Worcestershire sauce, toss well and transfer to a pan that fits your Air Fryer. Sprinkle breadcrumbs and paprika, add melted butter, place in your Air Fryer and cook at 320°F for 25 minutes, shaking halfway. Divide among plates and serve right away. Enjoy!

Nutrition: cal 200, fat 13, fiber 9, carbs 17, protein 19

105. Snapper Fillets and Veggies

Preparation time: 10 minutes **Cooking time:** 14 minutes **Servings:** 2
Ingredients:
- 2 red snapper fillets, boneless
- 1 tablespoon olive oil
- ½ cup red bell pepper, chopped
- ½ cup green bell pepper, chopped
- ½ cup leeks, chopped
- Salt and black pepper to the taste
- 1 teaspoon tarragon, dried
- A splash of white wine

Directions:
1. In a heatproof dish that fits your Air Fryer, mix fish fillets with salt, pepper, oil, green bell pepper, red bell pepper, leeks, tarragon and wine; toss well everything, introduce in preheated Air Fryer at 350°F and cook for 14 minutes, flipping fish fillets halfway.
2. Divide fish and veggies among plates and serve warm. Enjoy!

Nutrition: cal 300, fat 12, fiber 8, carbs 29, protein 12

106. Special Catfish Fillets

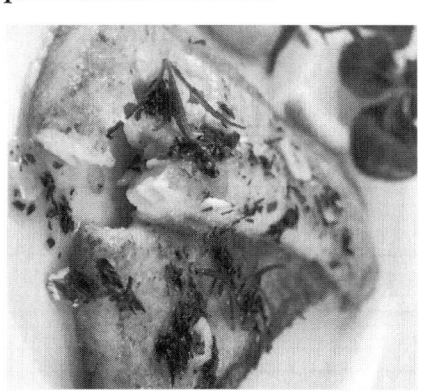

Preparation time: 13 minutes **Cooking time:** 12 minutes **Servings:** 4
Ingredients:
- 2 catfish fillets
- ½ teaspoon garlic, minced
- 2 ounces of butter
- 4 ounces Worcestershire sauce
- ½ teaspoon jerk seasoning
- 1 teaspoon mustard
- 1 tablespoon balsamic vinegar
- ¾ cup catsup
- Salt and black pepper to the taste
- 1 tablespoon parsley, chopped

Directions:
1. Heat a pan with the butter over medium heat, add Worcestershire sauce, garlic, jerk seasoning, mustard, catsup, vinegar, salt and pepper, stir well, take off the heat and add fish fillets.
2. Toss well, leave aside for 10 minutes, drain fillets, transfer them to your preheated Air Fryer's basket at 350°F and cook for 8 minutes, flipping fillets halfway.
3. Divide among plates, sprinkle parsley on top and serve right away. Enjoy!

Nutrition: cal 351, fat 8, fiber 16, carbs 27, protein 17

107. Squid and Guacamole

Preparation time: 10 minutes **Cooking time:** 6 minutes **Servings:** 2
Ingredients:
- 2 medium squids, tentacles separated and tubes scored lengthwise
- 1 tablespoon olive oil

- Juice from 1 lime
- Salt and black pepper to the taste

For the guacamole:
- 2 avocados, pitted, peeled and chopped
- 1 tablespoon coriander, chopped
- 2 red chilies, chopped
- 1 tomato, chopped
- 1 red onion, chopped
- Juice from 2 limes

Directions:
1. Season squid and squid tentacles with salt, and pepper, drizzle the olive oil all over, put in your Air Fryer's basket and cook at 360°F for 3 minutes on each side.
2. Transfer squid to a bowl, drizzle lime juice all over and toss.
3. Meanwhile, put avocado in a bowl, mash with a fork, add coriander, chilies, tomato, onion and juice from 2 limes and toss. Divide squid on plates, top with guacamole and serve. Enjoy!

Nutrition: calories 500, fat 43, fiber 6, carbs 7, protein 20

108. Stuffed Calamari

Preparation time: 14 minutes **Cooking time:** 25 minutes **Servings:** 4
Ingredients:
- 4 big calamari, tentacles separated and chopped, and tubes reserved
- 2 tablespoons parsley, chopped
- 5 ounces kale, chopped
- 2 garlic cloves, minced
- 1 red bell pepper, chopped
- 1 tablespoon olive oil
- 2 ounces of canned tomato puree
- 1 yellow onion, chopped
- Salt and black pepper to the taste

Directions:
1. Heat a pan with the oil over medium heat, add onion and garlic, stir and cook for 2 minutes. Add bell pepper, tomato puree, calamari tentacles, kale, salt and pepper, stir, cook for 10 minutes and take off the heat. Stir and cook for 3 minutes.
2. Stuff calamari tubes with this mix, secure them with toothpicks, put them in your Air Fryer and cook at 360°F for 20 minutes. Divide calamari on plates, sprinkle parsley all over and serve.
3. Enjoy!

Nutrition: cal 322, fat 10, fiber 14, carbs 14, protein 22

109. Swordfish and Mango Salsa

Preparation time: 10 minutes **Cooking time:** 6 minutes
Servings: 2
Ingredients:
- 2 medium swordfish steaks
- Salt and black pepper to the taste
- 2 teaspoons avocado oil
- 1 tablespoon cilantro, chopped
- 1 mango, chopped
- 1 avocado, pitted, peeled and chopped
- A pinch of cumin
- A pinch of onion powder
- A pinch of garlic powder
- 1 orange, peeled and sliced
- ½ tablespoon balsamic vinegar

Directions:
1. Season fish steaks with salt, pepper, garlic powder, onion powder and cumin and rub with half of the oil, place in your Air Fryer and cook at 360°F for 6 minutes, flipping halfway.
2. Meanwhile, mix avocado with mango, cilantro, balsamic vinegar, salt, pepper and the rest of the oil and stir well.
3. Divide fish on plates, top with mango salsa and serve with orange slices on the side.
4. Enjoy!

Nutrition: calories 200, fat 7, fiber 2, carbs 14, protein 14

110. Tilapia and Chives Sauce

Preparation time: 10 minutes **Cooking time:** 8 minutes
Servings: 4
Ingredients:
- 4 medium tilapia fillets
- Cooking spray
- Salt and black pepper to the taste
- 2 teaspoons honey
- ¼ cup Greek yogurt
- Juice from 1 lemon
- 2 tablespoons chives, chopped

Directions:
1. Season fish with salt and pepper, spray with cooking spray, place in preheated Air Fryer 350°F and cook for 8 minutes, flipping halfway.
2. Meanwhile, mix yogurt with honey, salt, pepper, chives and lemon juice and whisk well.
3. Divide Air Fryer fish on plates, drizzle yogurt sauce and serve immediately.
4. Enjoy!

Nutrition: cal 261, fat 8, fiber 18, carbs 24, protein 21

111. Trout Fillet and Orange Sauce

Preparation time: 12 minutes **Cooking time:** 10 minutes **Servings:** 4
Ingredients:
- 4 trout fillets, skinless and boneless
- 4 spring onions, chopped
- 1 tablespoon olive oil
- 1 tablespoon ginger, minced
- Salt and black pepper to the taste
- Juice and zest from 1 orange

Directions:
1. Season trout fillets with salt, and pepper, rub them with the olive oil; place in a pan that fits your Air Fryer; add ginger, green onions, orange
2. zest and juice, toss well, and place in your Air Fryer and cook at 360°F for 10 minutes.
3. Divide fish and sauce among plates and serve right away. Enjoy!

Nutrition: cal 239, fat 10, fiber 7, carbs 18, protein 23

112. Tuna and Chimichurri Sauce

Preparation time: 10 minutes **Cooking time:** 8 minutes
Servings: 4
Ingredients:
- ½ cup cilantro, chopped
- 1/3 cup olive oil+ 2 tablespoons
- 1 small red onion, chopped
- 3 tablespoons balsamic vinegar
- 2 tablespoons parsley, chopped
- 2 tablespoons basil, chopped
- 1 jalapeno pepper, chopped
- 1 pound sushi tuna steak
- Salt and black pepper to the taste
- 1 teaspoon red pepper flakes
- 1 teaspoon thyme, chopped
- 3 garlic cloves, minced
- 2 avocados, pitted, peeled and sliced
- 6 ounces of baby arugula

Directions:
1. Mix 1/3 cup oil with jalapeno, vinegar, onion, cilantro, basil, garlic, parsley, pepper flakes, thyme, salt and pepper, whisk well and leave aside for now.
2. Season tuna with salt and pepper and rub with the rest of the oil.
3. Place in your Air Fryer and cook at 360°F for 3 minutes on each side.
4. Mix arugula with half of the chimichurri mix you've made and toss to coat.
5. Divide arugula among plates, slice tuna and divide among plates, top with the rest of the chimichurri and serve.
6. Enjoy!

Nutrition: cal 276, fat 3, fiber 1, carbs 14, protein 20

POULTRY

113. Cheese Crusted Chicken

Preparation time: 13 minutes **Cooking time:** 15 minutes **Servings:** 4
Ingredients:
- 4 bacon slices, cooked and crumbled
- 4 chicken breasts, skinless and boneless
- 1 tablespoon water
- ½ cup avocado oil
- 1 egg, whisked
- Salt and black pepper to the taste
- 1 cup asiago cheese, shredded
- ¼ teaspoon garlic powder
- 1 cup parmesan cheese, grated

Directions:
1. Mix Parmesan with garlic, salt, and pepper in a bowl and stir. Mix Parmesan with garlic, salt, and pepper in a bowl and stir.
2. Combine the egg and water in another bowl and whisk until smooth. Add salt and pepper to the chicken and dip each piece into the egg and cheese mixture. Add the chicken to your fryer and cook at 320°F for 15 minutes.
3. Spread chicken on plates, sprinkle with bacon and Asiago cheese and serve. Enjoy!

Nutrition: cal 401, fat 22, fiber 12, carbs 32, protein 47

114. Chicken and Apricot Sauce

Preparation time: 11 minutes **Cooking time:** 20 minutes **Servings:** 4
Ingredients:
- 1 whole chicken, cut into medium pieces
- Salt and black pepper to the taste
- 1 tablespoon olive oil
- ½ teaspoon smoked paprika
- ¼ cup white wine
- ½ teaspoon marjoram, dried
- ¼ cup chicken stock
- 2 tablespoons white vinegar
- ¼ cup apricot preserves
- 1 and ½ teaspoons of ginger, grated
- 2 tablespoons honey

Directions:
1. Add salt, pepper, marjoram and paprika to the chicken, stir to coat, add oil, rub well, place in the air fryer and bake at 360°F for 10 minutes. Transfer the chicken into a saucepan suitable for your air fryer, add the broth, wine, vinegar, ginger, apricot jams and honey, and stir. Place your air fryer and cook at 360°F for another 10 minutes. Divide chicken and apricot sauce into platters and serve.
2. Enjoy!

Nutrition: cal 202, fat 7, fiber 19, carbs 20, protein 14

115. Chicken and Asparagus

Preparation time: 9 minutes **Cooking time:** 20 minutes **Servings:** 4
Ingredients:
- 8 chicken wings, halved
- 8 asparagus spears
- Salt and black pepper to the taste
- 1 tablespoon rosemary, chopped
- 1 teaspoon cumin, ground

Directions:
1. Pat dry the chicken wings, add salt, pepper, cumin and rosemary, place in your frying pan and bake at 360°F for 20 minutes.
2. Meanwhile, heat a skillet over medium heat, add the asparagus and water to cover, then steam a few minutes. Place in a bowl of ice water, drain and place on plates.
3. Arrange the chicken wings aside and serve.
4. Enjoy!

Nutrition: cal 271, fat 8, fiber 12, carbs 24, protein 22

116. Chicken and Creamy Mushrooms

Preparation time: 12 minutes **Cooking time:** 30 minutes **Servings:** 8
Ingredients:
- 8 chicken thighs
- Salt and black pepper to the taste
- 8 ounces cremini mushrooms, halved
- 3 garlic cloves, minced
- 3 tablespoons butter, melted
- 1 cup chicken stock
- ¼ cup heavy cream
- ½ teaspoon basil, dried
- ½ teaspoon thyme, dried
- ½ teaspoon oregano, dried
- 1 tablespoon mustard
- ¼ cup Parmesan, grated

Directions:
1. Rub the chicken pieces with two tablespoons of butter, season with salt and pepper, add to the basket of your fryer. Bake at 370°F for 5 minutes, then set aside in a bowl for now.
2. Meanwhile, heat a skillet with the remaining butter over medium-high heat, add the mushrooms and garlic, toss and cook for 5 minutes. Add salt, pepper, oregano, stock, thyme and basil, mix well and transfer to a heat-proof dish that fits your fryer.
3. Add chicken, mix well, add fryer and cook at 370°F for 20 minutes. Add mustard, Parmesan and thick cream, stir again, cook for another 5 minutes, divide among plates and serve.
4. Enjoy!

Nutrition: cal. 340, fat 10, fiber 13, carbs 22, protein 12

117. Chicken and Creamy Veggie Mix

Preparation time: 13 minutes **Cooking time:** 30 minutes **Servings:** 6
Ingredients:
- 2 cups whipping cream
- 40 ounces of chicken pieces, boneless and skinless
- 3 tablespoons butter, melted
- ½ cup yellow onion, chopped
- ¾ cup red peppers, chopped
- 29 ounces of chicken stock
- Salt and black pepper to the taste
- 1 bay leaf
- 8 ounces mushrooms, chopped
- 17 ounces of asparagus, trimmed
- 3 teaspoons thyme, chopped

Directions:
1. Heat a saucepan with butter on medium heat; add the onion and peppers; stir and cook for 3 minutes. Add bay leaf, broth, salt, pepper, bring to a boil and bake for ten minutes.
2. Add the asparagus, mushrooms, chicken, cream, thyme, salt and pepper to taste, toss, place in the air fryer and bake at 360°F for 15 minutes.
3. Divide chicken and vegetable mixture into platters and serve. Enjoy!

Nutrition: cal. 361, fat 27, fiber 13, carbs 24, protein 47

118. Chicken and Spinach Salad

Preparation time: 14 minutes **Cooking time:** 12 minutes **Servings:** 2
Ingredients:
- 2 teaspoons parsley, dried
- 2 chicken breasts, skinless and boneless
- ½ teaspoon onion powder
- 2 teaspoons sweet paprika
- ½ cup lemon juice
- Salt and black pepper to the taste
- 5 cups of baby spinach
- 8 strawberries, sliced
- 1 small red onion, sliced
- 2 tablespoons balsamic vinegar
- 1 avocado, pitted, peeled and chopped
- ¼ cup olive oil
- 1 tablespoon tarragon, chopped

Directions:
1. Put the chicken into a bowl, add the lemon juice, onion powder, parsley, and paprika and stir.
2. Transfer chicken to the air fryer and bake at 360°F for 12 minutes. Whisk together the spinach, onion, strawberries and avocado in a bowl.
3. Blend the oil with the vinegar, salt, pepper and tarragon in another bowl, whisk well, add to the salad and stir.
4. Place the chicken on the plates, add the spinach lettuce and serve. Enjoy!

Nutrition: cal 241, fat 5, fiber 13, carbs 25, protein 22

119. Chicken Breasts and BBQ Chili Sauce

Preparation time: 12 minutes **Cooking time:** 20 minutes **Servings:** 6
Ingredients:
- 2 cups chili sauce
- 2 cups ketchup
- 1 cup pear jelly
- ¼ cup honey

- ½ teaspoon liquid smoke
- 1 teaspoon chili powder
- 1 teaspoon mustard powder
- 1 teaspoon sweet paprika
- Salt and black pepper to the taste
- 1 teaspoon garlic powder
- 6 chicken breasts, skinless and boneless

Directions:
1. Add salt and pepper to chicken breasts, place in a preheated air fryer and bake in 350°F oven for 10 minutes.
2. Heat a frying pan with chili sauce over medium heat. Stir in ketchup, pear jelly, honey, liquid smoke, mustard powder, chili powder, sweet paprika, salt, pepper and garlic powder. Bring to a boil, then bake for 10 minutes.
3. Add the fried chicken breasts, mix thoroughly, divide among the plates and serve. Enjoy!

Nutrition: cal. 474, fat 13, fiber 7, carbs 39, protein 33

120. Chicken Cacciatore

Preparation time: 16 minutes **Cooking time:** 20 minutes **Servings:** 4
Ingredients:
- Salt and black pepper to the taste
- 8 chicken drumsticks, bone-in
- 1 bay leaf
- 1 teaspoon garlic powder
- 1 yellow onion, chopped
- 28 ounces canned tomatoes and juice, crushed
- 1 teaspoon oregano, dried
- ½ cup black olives, pitted and sliced

Directions:
1. Mix the chicken with the salt, pepper, garlic powder, bay leaf, onion, tomatoes and juice, oregano and olives in a heat-resistant pan suitable for your fryer.
2. Transfer to your preheated fryer and bake at 365°F for 20 minutes. Arrange plates and serve. Enjoy!

Nutrition: cal. 301, fat 12, fiber 8, carbs 20, protein 24

121. Chicken Parmesan

Preparation time: 12 minutes **Cooking time:** 15 minutes **Servings:** 4
Ingredients:
- 2 cups panko breadcrumbs
- ¼ cup parmesan, grated
- ½ teaspoon garlic powder
- 2 cups white flour
- 1 egg, whisked
- 1 and ½ pounds of chicken cutlets, skinless and boneless
- Salt and black pepper to the taste
- 1 cup mozzarella, grated
- 2 cups tomato sauce
- 3 tablespoons basil, chopped

Directions:
1. Blend the panko with the Parmesan and garlic powder and stir. Put the flour in another bowl and the egg in a third.
2. Add salt and pepper to the chicken, dip in the flour, egg mixture and panko. Put the chicken pieces in your air fryer and bake at 360°F for 3 minutes per side.
3. Transfer the chicken to an ovenproof pan that matches your fryer. Add the tomato sauce and top with the mozzarella, place over the air fryer and bake at 375°F for 7 minutes.
4. Divide between plates, sprinkle with basil and serve. Enjoy!

Nutrition: calor 304, fat 12, fiber 11, carbs 22, protein 15

122. Chinese Duck Legs

Preparation time: 10 minutes **Cooking time:** 36 minutes **Servings:** 2
Ingredients:
- 2 duck legs
- 2 dried chilies, chopped
- 1 tablespoon olive oil
- 2-star anise
- 1 bunch of spring onions, chopped
- 4 ginger slices
- 1 tablespoon oyster sauce
- 1 tablespoon soy sauce
- 1 teaspoon sesame oil
- 14 ounces of water
- 1 tablespoon rice wine

Directions:
1. Heat a saucepan with oil over medium-high heat. Add chili pepper, star anise, sesame oil, rice wine, ginger, soy sauce and oysters sauce and water.

2. Toss and bake for 6 minutes. Add spring onions and duck legs, toss and transfer to a frying pan suitable for your deep fryer.
3. Place in your deep fryer and bake at 370°F for 30 minutes. Divide among plates and serve.
4. Enjoy!

Nutrition: cal. 300, fat 12, fiber 12, carb 26, protein 18

123. Duck and Veggies

Preparation time: 9 minutes **Cooking time:** 20 minutes **Servings:** 8
Ingredients:
- 1 duck, chopped into medium pieces
- 3 cucumbers, chopped
- 3 tablespoons white wine
- 2 carrots, chopped
- 1 cup chicken stock
- 1 small ginger piece, grated
- Salt and black pepper to the taste

Directions:
1. Mix the duck pieces with the cucumbers, wine, carrots, ginger, stock, salt and pepper in a frying pan suitable for your fryer
2. Put in your Air Fryer and bake at 370°F for 20 minutes. Divide everything into plates and serve. Enjoy!

Nutrition: cal. 201, fat 10, fiber 8, carbs 20, protein 22

124. Duck Breasts and Mango Mix

Preparation time: 1-hour **Cooking time:** 10 minutes **Servings:** 4
Ingredients:
- 4 duck breasts
- 1 and ½ tablespoons lemongrass, chopped
- 3 tablespoons lemon juice
- 2 tablespoons olive oil
- Salt and black pepper to the taste
- 3 garlic cloves, minced

For the mango mix:
- 1 mango, peeled and chopped
- 1 tablespoon coriander, chopped
- 1 red onion, chopped
- 1 tablespoon sweet chili sauce
- 1 and ½ tablespoon of lemon juice
- 1 teaspoon ginger, grated
- ¾ teaspoon sugar

Directions:
1. Mix duck chests with salt, pepper, lemongrass, lemon juice, olive oil and garlic. Refrigerate for 1 hour, transfer to the frying pan and bake at 360°F for 10 minutes, turning once.
2. Meanwhile, combine the mango, cilantro, onion, chili sauce, lemon juice, ginger and sugar in a bowl and mix well.
3. Divide the duck in the plates, add the mango mixture on the side, then serve.
4. Enjoy!

Nutrition: cal 465, fat 11, fiber 4, carbs 29, protein 38

125. Duck Breasts and Raspberry Sauce

Preparation time: 16 minutes **Cooking time:** 15 minutes **Servings:** 4
Ingredients:
- 2 duck breasts, skin on and scored
- Salt and black pepper to the taste
- Cooking spray
- ½ teaspoon cinnamon powder
- ½ cup raspberries
- 1 tablespoon sugar
- 1 teaspoon red wine vinegar
- ½ cup water

Directions:
1. Add salt and pepper to the duck breasts, spray with cooking spray, place in the pre-heated air fryer skin side down and bake at 350°F for 10 minutes.
2. Heat pan with water over medium heat. Add raspberries, cinnamon, sugar and wine and toss. Bring to a boil, transfer to blender, purée and return to skillet.
3. Add the Air Fryer duck breast to the pan, mix to coat, place in the plates and serve immediately. Enjoy!

Nutrition: cal 457, fat 22, fiber 4, carbs 14, protein 45

126. Duck Breasts on Red Wine and Orange Sauce

Preparation time: 16 minutes **Cooking time:** 35 minutes **Servings:** 4
Ingredients:
- ½ cup honey
- 2 cups orange juice
- 4 cups of red wine
- 2 tablespoons sherry vinegar
- 2 cups chicken stock
- 2 teaspoons pumpkin pie spice
- 2 tablespoons butter
- 2 duck breasts, skin on and halved
- 2 tablespoons olive oil

- Salt and black pepper to the taste

Directions:
1. Heat a skillet with the orange juice over medium heat, add the honey, stir well and bake for 10 minutes.
2. Add the wine, vinegar, broth, pie spices and butter, stir well. Cook for 10 minutes more and remove the heat. Salt and pepper the duck breasts, brush them with olive oil, place in the preheated fryer at 370°F and bake for 7 minutes per side.
3. Divide between plates, drizzle with wine and orange juice and serve immediately.
4. Enjoy!

Nutrition: cal. 300, fat 8, fiber 12, carbs 24, protein 11

127. Easy Chicken Thighs and Baby Potatoes

Preparation time: 18 minutes **Cooking time:** 30 minutes **Servings:** 4

Ingredients:
- 8 chicken thighs
- 2 tablespoons olive oil
- 1 pound of baby potatoes, halved
- 2 teaspoons oregano, dried
- 2 teaspoons rosemary, dried
- ½ teaspoon sweet paprika
- Salt and black pepper to the taste
- 2 garlic cloves, minced
- 1 red onion, chopped
- 2 teaspoons thyme, chopped

Directions:
1. Mix chicken thighs with potatoes, salt, pepper, thyme, paprika, onion, rosemary, garlic, oregano and oil.
2. Toss to coat, spread everything in a heat-proof dish that fits your Air Fryer and bake at 400°F for 30 minutes, shaking halfway.
3. Divide among plates and serve.
4. Enjoy!

Nutrition: calor.364, fat 14, fiber 13, carbs 21, protein 34

128. Easy Duck Breasts with Lemon

Preparation time: 13 minutes **Cooking time:** 15 minutes **Servings:** 4

Ingredients:
- 4 duck breasts, skinless and boneless
- 4 garlic heads, peeled, tops cut off and quartered
- 2 tablespoons lemon juice
- Salt and black pepper to the taste
- ½ teaspoon lemon pepper
- 1 and ½ tablespoon olive oil

Directions:
1. Mix duck breasts with garlic, lemon juice, salt, pepper, lemon pepper and olive oil and toss everything.
2. Transfer duck and garlic to your Air Fryer and bake at 350°F for 15 minutes. Divide duck breasts and garlic among plates and serve.
3. Enjoy!

Nutrition: calories 200, fat 7, fiber 1, carbs 11, protein 17

129. Lemon Chicken

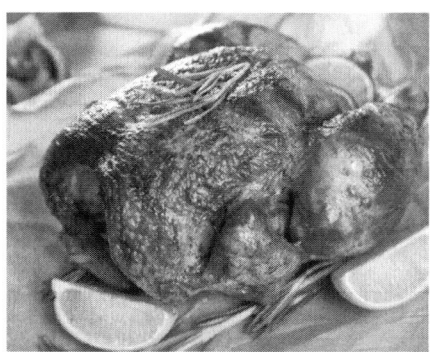

Preparation time: 11 minutes **Cooking time:** 30 minutes **Servings:** 6

Ingredients:
- 1 whole chicken, cut into medium pieces
- 1 tablespoon olive oil
- Salt and black pepper to the taste
- Juice from 2 lemons
- Zest from 2 lemons, grated

Directions:
1. Season chicken with salt, and pepper, rub with oil and lemon zest, drizzle lemon juice, put in your Air Fryer, bake at 350°F for 30 minutes, flipping chicken pieces halfway.
2. Divide among plates and serve with a side salad.
3. Enjoy!

Nutrition: cal. 334, fat 24, fiber 12, carbs 26, protein 20

130. Marinated Duck Breasts

Preparation time: 1 day **Cooking time:** 15 minutes **Servings:** 2

Ingredients:
- 2 duck breasts
- 1 cup white wine
- ¼ cup soy sauce
- 2 garlic cloves, minced
- 6 tarragon sprigs
- Salt and black pepper to the taste
- 1 tablespoon butter
- ¼ cup sherry wine

Directions:
1. Mix duck breasts with white wine, soy sauce, garlic, tarragon, salt and pepper, toss well and keep in the fridge for one day.
2. Transfer duck breasts to your preheated Air Fryer at 350°F and cook for 10 minutes, flipping halfway.
3. Meanwhile, pour the marinade into a pan, heat up over medium heat, add butter and sherry, stir, bring to a simmer, cook for 5 minutes and take off the heat.
4. Divide duck breasts on plates, drizzle the sauce all over and serve.
5. Enjoy!

Nutrition: cal. 475, fat 12, fiber 3, carbs 10, protein 48

131. Pepperoni Chicken

Preparation time: 10 minutes **Cooking time:** 22 minutes **Servings:** 6
Ingredients:
- 14 ounces tomato paste
- 1 tablespoon olive oil
- 4 medium chicken breasts, skinless and boneless
- Salt and black pepper to the taste
- 1 teaspoon oregano, dried
- 6 ounces mozzarella, sliced
- 1 teaspoon garlic powder
- 2 ounces pepperoni, sliced

Directions:
1. In a bowl, mix chicken with salt, pepper, garlic powder and oregano and toss.
2. Put chicken in your Air Fryer, cook at 350°F for 6 minutes and transfer to a pan that fits your Air Fryer.
3. Add mozzarella slices on top, spread tomato paste, top with pepperoni slices, introduce in your Air Fryer and cook at 350°F for 15 minutes more. Divide among plates and serve.
4. Enjoy!

Nutrition: cal 320, fat 10, fiber 16, carbs 23, protein 27

132. Turkey Quarters and Veggies

Preparation time: 14 minutes **Cooking time:** 34 minutes **Servings:** 4
Ingredients:
- 1 yellow onion, chopped
- 1 carrot, chopped
- 3 garlic cloves, minced
- 2 pounds turkey quarters
- 1 celery stalk, chopped
- 1 cup chicken stock
- 2 tablespoons olive oil
- 2 bay leaves
- ½ teaspoon rosemary, dried
- ½ teaspoon sage, dried
- ½ teaspoon thyme, dried
- Salt and black pepper to the taste

Directions:
1. Rub turkey quarters with salt, pepper, half of the oil, thyme, sage, rosemary and thyme, put in your Air Fryer and cook at 360°F for 20 minutes.
2. In a pan that fits your Air Fryer, mix the onion with carrot, garlic, celery, the rest of the oil, stock, bay leaves, salt and pepper and toss.
3. Add turkey, introduce everything in your Air Fryer and cook at 360°F for 14 minutes more. Divide everything into plates.
4. Enjoy!

Nutrition: cal 362, fat 12, fiber 16, carbs 22, protein 17

133. Turkey, Peas and Mushrooms Casserole

Preparation time: 10 minutes **Cooking time:** 20 minutes **Servings:** 4
Ingredients:
- 2 pounds turkey breasts, skinless, boneless
- Salt and black pepper to the taste
- 1 yellow onion, chopped
- 1 celery stalk, chopped
- ½ cup peas
- 1 cup chicken stock
- 1 cup cream of mushrooms soup
- 1 cup bread cubes

Directions:
1. In a pan that fits your Air Fryer, mix turkey with salt, pepper, onion, celery, peas and stock, introduce it to your Air Fryer and cook at 360°F for 15 minutes.
2. Add bread cubes and cream of mushroom soup, stir, toss and cook at 360°F for 5 minutes more.
3. Divide among plates and serve hot. Enjoy!

Nutrition: cal. 271, fat 9, fiber 9, carbs 16, protein 7

134. Veggie Stuffed Chicken Breasts

Preparation time: 13 minutes **Cooking time:** 15 minutes **Servings:** 4
Ingredients:
- 4 chicken breasts, skinless and boneless
- 2 tablespoons olive oil
- Salt and black pepper to the taste
- 1 zucchini, chopped
- 1 teaspoon Italian seasoning

- 2 yellow bell peppers, chopped
- 3 tomatoes, chopped
- 1 red onion, chopped
- 1 cup mozzarella, shredded

Directions:
1. Mix a slit on each chicken breast, creating a pocket, season with salt and pepper and rub them with olive oil.
2. In a bowl, mix zucchini with Italian seasoning, bell peppers, tomatoes and onion and stir.
3. Stuff chicken breasts with this mix, sprinkle mozzarella over them, place them in your Air Fryer's basket and cook at 350°F for 15 minutes. Divide among plates and serve. Enjoy!

Nutrition: calories 300, fat 12, fiber 7, carbs 22, protein 18

MEAT

135. Air Fried Sausage and Mushrooms

Preparation time: 12 minutes **Cooking time:** 40 minutes **Servings:** 6
Ingredients:
- 3 red bell peppers, chopped
- 2 pounds of pork sausage, sliced
- Salt and black pepper to the taste
- 2 pounds Portobello mushrooms, sliced
- 2 sweet onions, chopped
- 1 tablespoon brown sugar
- 1 teaspoon olive oil

Directions:
1. In a baking dish suitable for your Air Fryer, combine the sausage slices and oil, salt, pepper, bell pepper, mushrooms, onion and sugar and stir. Place in your Air Fryer and cook at 300°F for 40 minutes.
2. Divide among plates and serve right away. Enjoy!

Nutrition: cal. 132, fat 12, fiber 1, carbs 13, protein 18

136. Air Fryer Lamb Shanks

Preparation time: 14 minutes **Cooking time:** 45 minutes **Servings:** 4
Ingredients:
- 4 lamb shanks
- 1 yellow onion, chopped
- 1 tablespoon olive oil
- 4 teaspoons coriander seeds, crushed
- 2 tablespoons white flour
- 4 bay leaves
- 2 teaspoons honey
- 5 ounces dry sherry
- 2 and ½ cups of chicken stock
- Salt and pepper to the taste

Directions:
1. Add salt and pepper to the lamb shanks, rub with half the oil, place in the fryer and cook at 360°F for 10 minutes.
2. Heat a skillet that adapts to your air fryer with the remaining oil on medium-high heat; add the onion and cilantro, stir and cook for 5 minutes.
3. Add the flour, sherry, broth, honey, laurel leaves, salt and pepper, stir, simmer and add the lamb. Transfer everything to your fryer and cook at 360°F for 30 minutes.
4. Arrange on plates and serve. Enjoy!

Nutrition: cal. 284, fat 4, fiber 2, carbs 17, protein 26

137. Balsamic Beef

Preparation time: 10 minutes **Cooking time:** 1-hour
Servings: 6
Ingredients:
- 1 medium beef roast
- 1 tablespoon Worcestershire sauce
- ½ cup balsamic vinegar
- 1 cup beef stock
- 1 tablespoon honey
- 1 tablespoon soy sauce
- 4 garlic cloves, minced

Directions:
1. In a heat-proof dish that fits your Air Fryer, mix roast with Worcestershire sauce, vinegar, stock, honey, soy sauce and garlic, toss well, introduce to your Air Fryer and cook at 370°F for 1 hour.
2. Slice roast, divide among plates, drizzle the sauce and serve. Enjoy!

Nutrition: cal. 311, fat 7, fiber 12, carbs 20, protein 16

138. Beef Brisket and Onion Sauce

Preparation time: 13 minutes **Cooking time:** 2 hours
Servings: 6
Ingredients:
- 1-pound yellow onion, chopped
- 4 pounds of beef brisket

- 1 pound carrot, chopped
- 8 earl grey tea bags
- ½ pound celery, chopped
- Salt and black pepper to the taste
- 4 cups water

For the sauce:
- 16 ounces canned tomatoes, chopped
- ½ pound celery, chopped
- 1 ounce garlic, minced
- 4 ounces of vegetable oil
- 1-pound sweet onion, chopped
- 1 cup brown sugar
- 8 earl grey tea bags
- 1 cup white vinegar

Directions:
1. Place the water in a heat-resistant pan suitable for your fryer; add one pound onion, one pound carrot, half pound celery, salt and pepper.
2. Stir and sauté over medium-high heat. Add the beef breast and eight tea bags, toss, transfer to the deep fryer and cook at 300°F for 1 hour and 30 minutes.
3. Meanwhile, heat a skillet with the vegetable oil over medium-high heat; add 1 pound of onion, stir and brown for 10 minutes. Add garlic, half-pound celery, tomatoes, sugar, vinegar, salt, pepper and eight tea bags, stir, bring to a boil, bake for 10 minutes and discard the tea bags.
4. Transfer the brisket to a cutting board, slice, divide among the dishes, drizzle with the onion sauce and serve. Enjoy!

Nutrition: cal. 401, fat 12, fiber 4, carbs 38, protein 34

139. Beef Patties and Mushroom Sauce

Preparation time: 13 minutes **Cooking time:** 25 minutes **Servings:** 6
Ingredients:
- 2 pounds of beef, ground
- Salt and black pepper to the taste
- ½ teaspoon garlic powder
- 1 tablespoon soy sauce
- ¼ cup beef stock
- ¾ cup flour
- 1 tablespoon parsley, chopped
- 1 tablespoon onion flakes

For the sauce:
- 1 cup yellow onion, chopped
- 2 cups mushrooms, sliced
- 2 tablespoons bacon fat
- 2 tablespoons butter
- ½ teaspoon soy sauce
- ¼ cup sour cream
- ½ cup beef stock
- Salt and black pepper to the taste

Directions:
1. Mix the beef with the salt, pepper, garlic powder, a tablespoon of soy sauce, ¼ cup of beef stock, flour, parsley and onion flakes and mix well.
2. Form 6 patties, place in the fryer and cook at 350°F for 14 minutes. Meanwhile, heat a skillet with the butter and bacon fat over medium heat, add the mushrooms, toss and cook for 4 minutes.
3. Add the onions, stir and cook for an additional 4 minutes. Add half a teaspoon of soy sauce, sour cream and half a cup of broth, stir well, bring to a boil and remove the heat.
4. Divide the steak patties among the plates and serve with the mushroom sauce. Enjoy!

Nutrition: cal. 436, fat 23, fiber 4, carbs 6, protein 32

140. Beef Roast and Wine Sauce

Preparation time: 14 minutes **Cooking time:** 45 minutes **Servings:** 6
Ingredients:
- 3 pounds of beef roast
- Salt and black pepper to the taste
- 17 ounces of beef stock
- 3 ounces of red wine
- ½ teaspoon chicken salt
- ½ teaspoon smoked paprika
- 1 yellow onion, chopped
- 4 garlic cloves, minced
- 3 carrots, chopped
- 5 potatoes, chopped

Directions:
1. Mix the salt, pepper, chicken, salt and paprika, stir, rub the beef with this mixture and place it in a big pan that fits your fryer.
2. Add onion, garlic, broth, wine, potatoes and carrots. Introduce in your Air Fryer and bake at 360°F for 45 minutes. Divide everything into plates and serve. Enjoy!

Nutrition: cal. 305, fat 20, fiber 7, carbs 20, protein 32

141. Burgundy Beef Mix

Preparation time: 10 minutes **Cooking time: 1-hour Servings:** 7
Ingredients:
- 2 pounds beef chuck roast, cubed
- 15 ounces canned tomatoes, chopped
- 4 carrots, chopped
- Salt and black pepper to the taste

- ½ pounds mushrooms, sliced
- 2 celery ribs, chopped
- 2 yellow onions, chopped
- 1 cup beef stock
- 1 tablespoon thyme, chopped
- ½ teaspoon mustard powder
- 3 tablespoons almond flour
- 1 cup water

Directions:
1. Heat a heat-resistant pan that fits your air fryer over medium-high heat, add the beef, stir and fry for a few minutes.
2. Stir in tomatoes, mushrooms, onions, carrots, celery, salt, pepper, mustard, broth and thyme. In a bowl, combine the water and flour, mix well, add to the pan, mix, place in the pan and cook at 300°F for 1 hour.
3. Arrange in bowls and serve. Enjoy!

Nutrition: cal. 276, fat 13, fiber 4, carbs 17, protein 28

142. Creamy Pork

Preparation time: 17 minutes **Cooking time:** 22 minutes **Servings:** 6
Ingredients:
- 2 pounds of pork meat, boneless and cubed
- 2 yellow onions, chopped
- 1 tablespoon olive oil
- 1 garlic clove, minced
- 3 cups chicken stock
- 2 tablespoons sweet paprika
- Salt and black pepper to the taste
- 2 tablespoons white flour
- 1 and ½ cups sour cream
- 2 tablespoons dill, chopped

Directions:
1. In a frying pan that fits your fryer, mix the pork with the salt, pepper and oil, stir, place in your fryer and cook at 360°F for 7 minutes.
2. Add onion, garlic, broth, paprika, flour, sour cream and dill, stir and cook at 370°F for 15 minutes.
3. Divide everything into plates. Enjoy!

Nutrition: cal. 301, fat 4, fiber 10, carbs 26, protein 34

143. Crispy Lamb

Preparation time: 12 minutes **Cooking time:** 30 minutes **Servings:** 4
Ingredients:
- 1 tablespoon breadcrumbs
- 2 tablespoons macadamia nuts, toasted and crushed
- 1 tablespoon olive oil
- 1 garlic clove, minced
- 28 ounces rack of lamb
- Salt and black pepper to the taste
- 1 egg
- 1 tablespoon rosemary, chopped

Directions:
1. Mix oil with garlic in a bowl and stir well.
2. Season lamb with salt and pepper and brush with the oil. Mix nuts with breadcrumbs and rosemary in another bowl.
3. Soak the lamb in the egg, then in the macadamia mixture, place them in your fryer's basket, cook at 360°F and cook for 25 minutes.
4. Increase temperature to 400°F and cook for another 5 minutes.
5. Divide between plates and serve immediately. Enjoy!

Nutrition: cal. 231, fat 2, fiber 2, carbs 10, protein 12

144. Fennel Flavored Pork Roast

Preparation time: 10 minutes **Cooking time:** 1-hour **Servings:** 10
Ingredients:
- 1 and ½ pounds of pork loin roast, trimmed
- Salt and black pepper to the taste
- 3 garlic cloves, minced
- 2 tablespoons rosemary, chopped
- 1 teaspoon fennel, ground
- 1 tablespoon fennel seeds
- 2 teaspoons red pepper, crushed
- ¼ cup olive oil

Directions:
1. In a food processor, mix the garlic with the fennel seeds, rosemary, red pepper, a little black pepper and olive oil and stir until you get a paste.
2. Spread two tablespoons of garlic dough over the pork loin and rub thoroughly. Add salt and pepper, place in a pre-heated air pan and cook at 350°F for 30 minutes.

3. Lower heat to 300°F and cook another 15 minutes. Slice pork and divide among plates. Enjoy!

Nutrition: cal. 301, fat 14, fiber 9, carbs 26, protein 22

145. Filet Mignon and Mushrooms Sauce

Preparation time: 14 minutes **Cooking time:** 25 minutes **Servings:** 4
Ingredients:
- 12 mushrooms, sliced
- 1 shallot, chopped
- 4 fillet mignons
- 2 garlic cloves, minced
- 2 tablespoons olive oil
- ¼ cup Dijon mustard
- ¼ cup wine
- 1 and ¼ cup coconut cream
- 2 tablespoons parsley, chopped
- Salt and black pepper to the taste

Directions:
1. Heat a pan with the oil over medium-high heat; add garlic and shallots, stir and cook for 3 minutes.
2. Add the mushrooms, stir and bake for 4 minutes more.
3. Add wine, stir and cook until it evaporates.
4. Add coconut cream, mustard, parsley, a pinch of salt and black pepper to the taste, stir, cook for 6 minutes more and take off the heat.
5. Season fillets with salt and pepper, put them in your Air Fryer and bake at 360°F for 10 minutes.
6. Divide fillets among plates and serve with the mushroom sauce. Enjoy!

Nutrition: cal. 340, fat 12, fiber 1, carbs 14, protein 23

146. Flavored Rib Eye Steak

Preparation time: 16 minutes **Cooking time:** 20 minutes **Servings:** 4
Ingredients:
- 2 pounds rib-eye steak
- Salt and black pepper to the taste
- 1 tablespoon olive oil

For the rub:
- 3 tablespoons sweet paprika
- 2 tablespoons onion powder
- 2 tablespoons garlic powder
- 1 tablespoon brown sugar
- 2 tablespoons oregano, dried
- 1 tablespoon cumin, ground
- 1 tablespoon rosemary, dried

Directions:
1. Mix paprika with onion and garlic powder, sugar, oregano, rosemary, salt, pepper and cumin; stir and rub steak with this mix.
2. Season steak with salt and pepper, rub again with the oil, put in your Air Fryer and cook in at 400°F for 20 minutes, flipping them halfway.
3. Transfer steak to a cutting board, slice and serve with a side salad. Enjoy!

Nutrition: calories 320, fat 8, fiber 7, carbs 22, protein 21

147. Lamb and Creamy Brussels Sprouts

Preparation time: 17 minutes **Cooking time:** 1 hour and 12 minutes **Servings:** 4
Ingredients:
- 2 pounds of lamb leg, marked
- 2 tablespoons olive oil
- 1 tablespoon of chopped rosemary
- 1 tablespoon lemon thyme, chopped
- 1 garlic clove, minced
- 1 and ½ pounds of Brussels sprouts, trimmed
- 1 tablespoon butter, melted
- ½ cup sour cream
- Salt and black pepper to the taste

Directions:
1. Sprinkle the lamb with salt, pepper, thyme, and rosemary, and brush with oil. Put into your fryer basket, cook at 300°F for 1 hour, Place on a plate and keep warm.
2. Combine Brussels sprouts with salt, pepper, garlic, butter and sour cream in a frying pan that suits your fryer. Place the fryer and cook at 400°F for 10 minutes. Arrange the lamb in the plates, add the Brussels sprouts to the side and serve. Enjoy!

Nutrition: calories 441, fat 23, fiber 0, carbs 2, protein 49

148. Lamb and Lemon Sauce

Preparation time: 13 minutes **Cooking time:** 30 minutes **Servings:** 4
Ingredients:
- 2 lamb shanks
- Salt and black pepper to the taste
- 2 garlic cloves, minced
- 4 tablespoons olive oil
- Juice from ½ lemon
- Zest from ½ lemon
- ½ teaspoon oregano, dried

Directions:
1. Salt and pepper the lamb, rub with the garlic, put into the deep fryer and cook at 350°F for 30

minutes. Meanwhile, in a bowl, mix lemon juice and the lemon peel, a little salt and pepper, olive oil, oregano and whisk very well.
2. Shred lamb, discard bone, divide among plates, and drizzle the lemon dressing. Enjoy!

Nutrition: calories 261, fat 7, fiber 3, carbs 15, protein 12

149. Lamb Shanks and Carrots

Preparation time: 14 minutes **Cooking time:** 45 minutes **Servings:** 4

Ingredients:
- 4 lamb shanks
- 2 tablespoons olive oil
- 1 yellow onion, finely chopped
- 6 carrots, roughly chopped
- 2 garlic cloves, minced
- 2 tablespoons tomato paste
- 1 teaspoon oregano, dried
- 1 tomato, roughly chopped
- 2 tablespoons water
- 4 ounces of red wine
- Salt and black pepper to the taste

Directions:
1. Add salt and pepper to the lamb, rub with the oil, place in the air fryer and cook at 360°F for 10 minutes. In a skillet suitable for your fryer, combine onion with carrots, garlic, tomato, oregano, tomato paste, wine, water and stir.
2. Add the lamb, mix and pour into the fryer and cook at 370°F for 35 minutes. Place in plates and serve. Enjoy!

Nutrition: cal. 433, fat 17, fiber 8, carbs 17, protein 43

150. Mediterranean Steaks and Scallops

Preparation time: 10 minutes **Cooking time:** 14 minutes **Servings:** 2

Ingredients:
- 10 sea scallops
- 2 beef steaks
- 4 garlic cloves, minced
- 1 shallot, chopped
- 2 tablespoons lemon juice
- 2 tablespoons parsley, chopped
- 2 tablespoons basil, chopped
- 1 teaspoon lemon zest
- ¼ cup butter
- ¼ cup veggie stock
- Salt and black pepper to the taste

Directions:
1. Season steaks with salt and pepper, put them in your Air Fryer, cook at 360°F for 10 minutes and transfer to a pan that fits the fryer.
2. Add shallot, garlic, butter, stock, basil, lemon juice, parsley, lemon zest and scallops, toss everything gently and bake at 360°F for 4 minutes.
3. Divide steaks and scallops among plates and serve. Enjoy!

Nutrition: calories 150, fat 2, fiber 2, carbs 14, protein 17

151. Pork Chops and Roasted Peppers

Preparation time: 15 minutes **Cooking time:** 16 minutes **Servings:** 4

Ingredients:
- 3 tablespoons olive oil
- 3 tablespoons lemon juice
- 1 tablespoon smoked paprika
- 2 tablespoons thyme, chopped
- 3 garlic cloves, minced
- 4 pork chops, bone-in
- Salta and black pepper to the taste
- 2 roasted bell peppers, chopped

Directions:
1. In a pan suitable for your Air Fryer, mix pork chops with oil, lemon juice, smoked paprika, thyme, garlic, bell peppers, salt and pepper; toss well, introduce in your Air Fryer and cook at 400°F for 16 minutes.
2. Divide pork chops and peppers, mix on plates and serve right away. Enjoy!

Nutrition: calories 321, fat 6, fiber 8, carbs 14, protein 17

152. Roasted Pork Belly and Apple Sauce

Preparation time: 16 minutes **Cooking time:** 40 minutes **Servings:** 6

Ingredients:
- 2 tablespoons sugar
- 1 tablespoon lemon juice
- 1-quart water
- 17 ounces of apples, cored and cut into wedges
- 2 pounds pork belly, scored
- Salt and black pepper to the taste
- A drizzle of olive oil

Directions:
1. Mix the water with the apples, lemon juice and sugar, in your mixer, mix well, transfer to a bowl, add the meat, mix well and drain.
2. Turn on the air fryer and cook at 400°F for 40 minutes. Place the sauce in a saucepan, heat over medium heat and simmer for 15 minutes.
3. Slice pork breast, divide on plates, drizzle with sauce and serve. Enjoy!

Nutrition: cal. 457, fat 34, fiber 4, carbs 10, protein 25

153. Short Ribs and Beer Sauce

Preparation time: 17 minutes **Cooking time:** 45 minutes **Servings:** 6
Ingredients:
- 4 pounds of short ribs, cut into small pieces
- 1 yellow onion, chopped
- Salt and black pepper to the taste
- ¼ cup tomato paste
- 1 cup dark beer
- 1 cup chicken stock
- 1 bay leaf
- 6 thyme springs, chopped
- 1 Portobello mushroom, dried

Directions:
1. Heat a skillet that works for your air fryer over medium heat; add the tomato paste, onion, broth, beer, bay leaves, mushrooms and thyme and bring to a boil.
2. Add the ribs to the fryer and bake at 350°F for 40 minutes. Arrange on plates and serve. Enjoy!

Nutrition: calories 301, fat 7, fiber 8, carbs 18, protein 23

154. Simple Air Fried Pork Shoulder

Preparation time: 35 minutes **Cooking time:** 1 hour and 20 minutes **Servings:** 6
Ingredients:
- 3 tablespoons garlic, minced
- 3 tablespoons olive oil
- 4 pounds of pork shoulder
- Salt and black pepper to the taste

Directions:
1. Blend the olive oil with the salt, pepper and oil, whisk well and brush the pork shoulder with this mixture. Transfer to the preheated air fryer and bake at 390°F for 10 minutes.
2. Reduce heat to 300 degrees Fahrenheit and roast pork for 1 hour and 10 minutes.
3. Slice the pork shoulder, arrange on the plates and serve with a side salad. Enjoy!

Nutrition: calories 221, fat 4, fiber 4, carbs 7, protein 10

155. Sirloin Steaks and Pico De Gallo

Preparation time: 13 minutes **Cooking time:** 10 minutes **Servings:** 4
Ingredients:
- 2 tablespoons chili powder
- 4 medium sirloin steaks
- 1 teaspoon cumin, ground
- ½ tablespoon sweet paprika
- 1 teaspoon onion powder
- 1 teaspoon garlic powder
- Salt and black pepper to the taste

For the Pico de Gallo:
- 1 small red onion, chopped
- 2 tomatoes, chopped
- 2 garlic cloves, minced
- 2 tablespoons lime juice
- 1 small green bell pepper, chopped
- 1 jalapeno, chopped
- ¼ cup cilantro, chopped
- ¼ teaspoon cumin, ground

Directions:
1. Mix chili powder with a pinch of salt, black pepper, onion powder, garlic powder, paprika and 1 teaspoon cumin, stir well, season steaks with this mix, put them in your Air Fryer and cook at 360°F for 10 minutes.
2. Mix the red onion with tomatoes, garlic, lime juice, bell pepper, jalapeno, cilantro, and black pepper to the taste and ¼ teaspoon cumin and toss.
3. Top steaks with this mix and serve. Enjoy!

Nutrition: cal. 200, fat 12, fiber 4, carbs 15, protein 18

156. Stuffed Pork Steaks

Preparation time: 12 minutes **Cooking time:** 20 minutes **Servings:** 4
Ingredients:
- Zest from 2 limes, grated
- Zest from 1 orange, grated
- Juice from 1 orange
- Juice from 2 limes
- 4 teaspoons garlic, minced
- ¾ cup olive oil
- 1 cup cilantro, chopped
- 1 cup mint, chopped
- 1 teaspoon oregano, dried
- Salt and black pepper to the taste
- 2 teaspoons cumin, ground
- 4 pork loin steaks

- 2 pickles, chopped
- 4 ham slices
- 6 Swiss cheese slices
- 2 tablespoons mustard

Directions:
1. Mix lime zest and juice with orange zest and juice, garlic, oil, cilantro, mint, oregano, cumin, salt and pepper in your food processor, and blend well.
2. Season steaks with salt and pepper, place them into a bowl, add marinade and toss to coat.
3. Place steaks on a working surface, divide pickles, cheese, mustard and ham, and roll and secure with toothpicks.
4. Put stuffed pork steaks in your Air Fryer and cook at 340°F for 20 minutes.
5. Divide among plates and serve with a side salad.
6. Enjoy!

Nutrition: calories 270, fat 7, fiber 2, carbs 13, protein 20

VEGETABLES

157. Air Fried Asparagus

Preparation time: 13 minutes **Cooking time:** 15 minutes **Servings:** 4
Ingredients:
- 2 pounds fresh asparagus, trimmed
- ¼ cup olive oil
- Salt and black pepper to the taste
- 1 teaspoon lemon zest
- 4 garlic cloves, minced
- ½ teaspoon oregano, dried
- ¼ teaspoon red pepper flakes
- 4 ounces feta cheese, crumbled
- 2 tablespoons parsley, finely chopped
- Juice from 1 lemon

Directions:
1. Mix oil with lemon zest, garlic, pepper flakes and oregano and whisk in a bowl.
2. Add asparagus, cheese, salt and pepper, and toss. Transfer to your Air Fryer's basket and bake at 350°F for 8 minutes.
3. Divide asparagus on plates, drizzle lemon juice and sprinkle parsley on top and serve. Enjoy!

Nutrition: cal. 162, fat 13, fiber 5, carbs 12, protein 8

158. Air Fried Leeks

Preparation time: 7 minutes **Cooking time:** 7 minutes **Servings:** 4
Ingredients:
- 4 leeks, washed, tips cut and halved
- Salt and black pepper to the taste
- 1 tbsp butter, melted
- 1 tbsp lemon juice

Directions:
1. Rub the leeks with the melted butter and season with salt and pepper. Put into your fair ryer and bake at 350°F for 7 minutes.
2. Transfer to a serving dish, pour in the lemon juice and serve. Enjoy!

Nutrition: calories 101, fat 4, fiber 2, carbs 6, protein 2

159. Balsamic Artichokes

Preparation time: 11 minutes **Cooking time:** 7 minutes **Servings:** 4
Ingredients:
- 4 big artichokes, trimmed
- Salt and black pepper to the taste
- 2 tablespoons lemon juice
- ¼ cup extra virgin olive oil
- 2 teaspoons balsamic vinegar
- 1 teaspoon oregano, dried
- 2 garlic cloves, minced

Directions:
1. Add salt and pepper to the artichokes and rub them with half the oil and half the lemon juice.
2. Put them in your air fryer and bake at 360 °F for 7 minutes. Meanwhile, in a bowl, combine the remaining lemon juice with the vinegar, salt, pepper, garlic and oregano remaining oil and stir to combine.
3. Place the artichokes on a plate, sprinkle with the balsamic vinaigrette and serve. Enjoy!

Nutrition: calories 201, fat 3, fiber 6, carbs 12, protein 4

160. Beets and Arugula Salad

Preparation time: 12 minutes **Cooking time:** 10 minutes **Servings:** 4
Ingredients:
- 1 and ½ pounds of beets, peeled and quartered
- A drizzle of olive oil
- 2 teaspoons orange zest, grated
- 2 tablespoons cider vinegar
- ½ cup orange juice

- 2 tablespoons brown sugar
- 2 scallions, chopped
- 2 teaspoons mustard
- 2 cups arugula

Directions:
1. Rub the beets with the oil and orange juice, put them in your fryer and bake at 350°F for 10 minutes.
2. Transfer the beetroot wedges to a bowl, add the green onions, arugula and orange peel and stir.
3. Combine the sugar, mustard and vinegar, whisk well, add to the salad in another bowl and mix. Enjoy!

Nutrition: calories 122, fat 2, fiber 3, carbs 11, protein 4

161. Broccoli and Tomatoes Air Fried Stew

Preparation time: 13 minutes **Cooking time:** 20 minutes **Servings:** 4

Ingredients:
- 1 broccoli head, florets separated
- 2 teaspoons coriander seeds
- 1 tablespoon olive oil
- 1 yellow onion, chopped
- Salt and black pepper to the taste
- A pinch of red pepper, crushed
- 1 small ginger piece, chopped
- 1 garlic clove, minced
- 28 ounces of canned tomatoes, pureed

Directions:
1. Heat a pan that fits your Air Fryer with the oil over medium heat; add onions, salt, pepper and red pepper; stir and cook for 7 minutes.
2. Add ginger, garlic, coriander seeds, tomatoes and broccoli, stir, introduce in your Air Fryer and bake at 360°F for 12 minutes.
3. Divide into bowls and serve.
4. Enjoy!

Nutrition: calories 150, fat 4, fiber 2, carbs 7, protein 12

162. Brussels Sprouts and Tomatoes Mix

Preparation time: 9 minutes **Cooking time:** 10 minutes **Servings:** 4

Ingredients:
- 1 pound Brussels sprouts, trimmed
- Salt and black pepper to the taste
- 6 cherry tomatoes, halved
- ¼ cup green onions, chopped
- 1 tablespoon olive oil

Directions:
1. Season Brussels sprouts with salt and pepper, put them in your Air Fryer and cook at 350°F for 10 minutes.
2. Transfer them to a bowl, add salt, pepper, cherry tomatoes, green onions and olive oil, toss well and serve.
3. Enjoy!

Nutrition: calories 121, fat 4, fiber 4, carbs 11, protein 4

163. Eggplant and Garlic Sauce

Preparation time: 11 minutes **Cooking time:** 10 minutes **Servings:** 4

Ingredients:
- 2 tablespoons olive oil
- 2 garlic cloves, minced
- 3 eggplants, halved and sliced
- 1 red chili pepper, chopped
- 1 green onion stalk, chopped
- 1 tablespoon ginger, grated
- 1 tablespoon soy sauce
- 1 tablespoon balsamic vinegar

Directions:
1. Heat a pan that fits your Air Fryer with the oil over medium-high heat, add eggplant slices and cook for 2 minutes.
2. Add chili pepper, garlic, green onions, ginger, soy sauce and vinegar, introduce to your Air Fryer and cook at 320°F for 7 minutes.
3. Divide among plates and serve. Enjoy!

Nutrition: calories 130, fat 2, fiber 4, carbs 7, protein 9

164. Eggplant Hash

Preparation time: 19 minutes **Cooking time:** 10 minutes **Servings:** 4

Ingredients:
- 1 eggplant, roughly chopped
- ½ cup olive oil
- ½ pound cherry tomatoes halved
- 1 teaspoon Tabasco sauce
- ¼ cup basil, chopped
- ¼ cup mint, chopped
- Salt and black pepper to the taste

Directions:
1. Heat a pan that fits your Air Fryer with half of the oil over medium-high heat, add eggplant pieces, cook for 3 minutes, flip, cook them for 3 minutes more and transfer to a bowl.
2. Heat the same pan with the rest of the oil over medium-high heat, add tomatoes, stir and cook for 1-2 minutes.

3. Return eggplant pieces to the pan, add salt, black pepper, basil, mint and Tabasco sauce, introduce in your Air Fryer and cook at 320°F for 6 minutes.
4. Divide among plates and serve. Enjoy!

Nutrition: calories 120, fat 1, fiber 4, carbs 8, protein 15

165. Flavored Air Fried Tomatoes

Preparation time: 10 minutes **Cooking time:** 15
Servings: 8
Ingredients:
- 1 jalapeno pepper, chopped
- 4 garlic cloves, minced
- 2 pounds cherry tomatoes, halved
- Salt and black pepper to the taste
- ¼ cup olive oil
- ½ teaspoon oregano, dried
- ¼ cup basil, chopped
- ½ cup parmesan, grated

Directions:
1. Mix tomatoes with garlic, and jalapeno, season with salt, pepper and oregano, drizzle the oil, toss to coat, introduce in your Air Fryer and cook at 380°F for 15 minutes.
2. Put tomatoes in a bowl, add basil and Parmesan, toss and serve. Enjoy!

Nutrition: calories 140, fat 2, fiber 2, carbs 6, protein 8

166. Flavored Fennel

Preparation time: 10 minutes **Cooking time:** 8 minutes
Servings: 4
Ingredients:
- 2 fennel bulbs, cut into quarters
- 3 tablespoons olive oil
- Salt and black pepper to the taste
- 1 garlic clove, minced
- 1 red chili pepper, chopped
- ¾ cup veggie stock
- Juice from ½ lemon
- ¼ cup white wine
- ¼ cup parmesan, grated

Directions:
1. Heat a pan that fits your Air Fryer with the oil over medium-high heat, add garlic and chili pepper, stir and cook for 2 minutes.
2. Add fennel, salt, pepper, stock, wine, lemon juice, and parmesan, toss to coat, introduce in your Air Fryer and cook at 350°F for 6 minutes.
3. Divide among plates. Enjoy!

Nutrition: calories 100, fat 4, fiber 8, carbs 4, protein 4

167. Flavored Green Beans

Preparation time: 12 minutes **Cooking time:** 15 minutes **Servings:** 4
Ingredients:
- 1-pound red potatoes, cut into wedges
- 1-pound green beans
- 2 garlic cloves, minced
- 2 tablespoons olive oil
- Salt and black pepper to the taste
- ½ teaspoon oregano, dried

Directions:
1. In a pan that fits your Air Fryer, combine potatoes with green beans, garlic, oil, salt, pepper and oregano, toss, introduce it to your Air Fryer and bake at 380°F for 15 minutes.
2. Divide among plates and serve.
3. Enjoy!

Nutrition: calories 211, fat 6, fiber 7, carbs 8, protein 5

168. Garlic Tomatoes

Preparation time: 13 minutes **Cooking time:** 15 minutes **Servings:** 4
Ingredients:
- 4 garlic cloves, crushed
- 1-pound mixed cherry tomatoes
- 3 thyme springs, chopped
- Salt and black pepper to the taste
- ¼ cup olive oil

Directions:
1. In a bowl, mix tomatoes with salt, black pepper, garlic, olive oil and thyme, toss to coat, introduce in your Air Fryer and bake at 360°F for 15 minutes.
2. Divide tomato mix among plates.
3. Enjoy!

Nutrition: calories 100, fat 0, fiber 1, carbs 1, protein 6

169. Green Beans and Parmesan

Preparation time: 10 minutes **Cooking time:** 8 minutes
Servings: 4
Ingredients:
- 12 ounces of green beans
- 2 teaspoons garlic, minced
- 2 tablespoons olive oil
- Salt and black pepper to the taste
- 1 egg, whisked
- 1/3 cup parmesan, grated

Directions:
1. Mix oil with salt, pepper, garlic and egg and whisk well.
2. Add green beans to this mix, toss well and sprinkle parmesan.
3. Transfer green beans to your Air Fryer and cook them at 390°F for 8 minutes.
4. Divide green beans into plates. Enjoy!

Nutrition: calories 120, fat 8, fiber 2, carbs 7, protein 4

170. Herbed Eggplant and Zucchini Mix

Preparation time: 10 minutes **Cooking time:** 8 minutes
Servings: 4
Ingredients:
- 1 eggplant, roughly cubed
- 3 zucchinis, roughly cubed
- 2 tablespoons lemon juice
- Salt and black pepper to the taste
- 1 teaspoon thyme, dried
- 1 teaspoon oregano, dried
- 3 tablespoons olive oil

Directions:
1. Put eggplant in a dish that fits your Air Fryer, add zucchini, lemon juice, salt, pepper, thyme, oregano and olive oil, toss, introduce to your Air Fryer and cook at 360°F for 8 minutes.
2. Divide among plates. Enjoy!

Nutrition: calories 152, fat 5, fiber 7, carbs 19, protein 5

171. Okra and Corn Salad

Preparation time: 12 minutes **Cooking time:** 12 minutes **Servings:** 6
Ingredients:
- 1 pound okra, trimmed
- 6 scallions, chopped
- 3 green bell peppers, chopped
- Salt and black pepper to the taste
- 2 tablespoons olive oil
- 1 teaspoon of sugar
- 28 ounces canned tomatoes, chopped
- 1 cup of corn

Directions:
1. Heat a pan that fits your Air Fryer with the oil over medium-high heat, add scallions and bell peppers, and stir and cook for 5 minutes.
2. Add okra, salt, pepper, sugar, tomatoes and corn, stir, introduce in your Air Fryer and bake at 360°F for 7 minutes.
3. Divide okra mix on plates and serve warm. Enjoy!

Nutrition: calories 152, fat 4, fiber 3, carbs 18, protein 4

172. Peppers Stuffed with Beef

Preparation time: 14 minutes **Cooking time:** 55 minutes **Servings:** 4
Ingredients:
- 1 pound beef, ground
- 1 teaspoon coriander, ground
- 1 onion, chopped
- 3 garlic cloves, minced
- 2 tablespoons olive oil
- 1 tablespoon ginger, grated
- ½ teaspoon cumin, ground
- ½ teaspoon turmeric powder
- 1 tablespoon hot curry powder
- Salt and black pepper to the taste
- 1 egg
- 4 bell peppers, cut into halves and seeds removed
- 1/3 cup raisins
- 1/3 cup walnuts, chopped

Directions:
1. Heat a pan with the oil over medium-high heat, add onion, stir and cook for 4 minutes.
2. Add garlic and beef, stir and cook for 10 minutes.
3. Add coriander, ginger, cumin, curry powder, salt, pepper, turmeric, walnuts and raisins, stir, take off the heat and mix with the egg.
4. Stuff pepper halves with this mix, introduce them to your Air Fryer and cook at 320°F for 20 minutes. Divide among plates and serve. Enjoy!

Nutrition: calories 170, fat 4, fiber 3, carbs 7, protein 12

173. Portobello Mushrooms

Preparation time: 11 minutes **Cooking time:** 12 minutes **Servings:** 4
Ingredients:
- 10 basil leaves
- 1 cup baby spinach
- 3 garlic cloves, chopped

- 1 cup almonds, roughly chopped
- 1 tablespoon parsley
- ¼ cup olive oil
- 8 cherry tomatoes, halved
- Salt and black pepper to the taste
- 4 Portobello mushrooms, stems removed and chopped

Directions:
1. In your food processor, mix basil with spinach, garlic, almonds, parsley, oil, salt, and black pepper to the taste and mushroom stems and blend well.
2. Stuff each mushroom with this mix, place them in your Air Fryer and cook at 350°F for 12 minutes.
3. Divide mushrooms into plates and serve.
4. Enjoy!

Nutrition: calories 145, fat 3, fiber 2, carbs 6, protein 17

174. Rutabaga and Cherry Tomatoes Mix

Preparation time: 14 minutes **Cooking time:** 15 minutes **Servings:** 4
Ingredients:
- 1 tablespoon shallot, chopped
- 1 garlic clove, minced
- ¾ cup cashews, soaked for a couple of hours and drained
- 2 tablespoons nutritional yeast
- ½ cup veggie stock
- Salt and black pepper to the taste
- 2 teaspoons lemon juice

For the pasta:
- 1 cup cherry tomatoes, halved
- 5 teaspoons olive oil
- ¼ teaspoon garlic powder
- 2 rutabagas, peeled and cut into thick noodles

Directions:
1. Place tomatoes and rutabaga noodles into a pan that fits your Air Fryer and drizzle the oil over them. Add salt, black pepper and garlic powder, toss to coat and bake in your Air Fryer at 350°F for 15 minutes.
2. Meanwhile, in a food processor, mix garlic with shallots, cashews, veggie stock, nutritional yeast, lemon juice, a touch of sea salt and black pepper to the taste and blend well.
3. Divide rutabaga pasta among plates, top with tomatoes, and drizzle the sauce over them. Enjoy!

Nutrition: calories 160, fat 2, fiber 5, carbs 10, protein 8

175. Spicy Cabbage

Preparation time: 10 minutes **Cooking time:** 8 minutes
Servings: 4
Ingredients:
- 1 cabbage, cut into 8 wedges
- 1 tablespoon sesame seed oil
- 1 carrot, grated
- ¼ cup apple cider vinegar
- ¼ cups apple juice
- ½ teaspoon cayenne pepper
- 1 teaspoon red pepper flakes, crushed

Directions:
1. In a pan that fits your Air Fryer, combine cabbage with oil, carrot, vinegar, apple juice, cayenne, and pepper flakes, toss, introduce in preheated Air Fryer and cook at 350°F for 8 minutes.
2. Divide cabbage mix among plates. Enjoy!

Nutrition: calories 100, fat 4, fiber 2, carbs 11, protein 7

176. Spinach Pie

Preparation time: 13 minutes **Cooking time:** 15 minutes **Servings:** 4
Ingredients:
- 7 ounces flour
- 2 tablespoons butter
- 7 ounces of spinach
- 1 tablespoon olive oil
- 2 eggs
- 2 tablespoons milk
- 3 ounces cottage cheese
- Salt and black pepper to the taste
- 1 yellow onion, chopped

Directions:
1. In your food processor, mix flour with butter, 1 egg, milk, salt and pepper, blend well, transfer to a bowl, knead, cover and leave for 10 minutes.
2. Heat a pan with the oil over medium-high heat, add onion and spinach, stir and cook for 2 minutes.

3. Add salt, pepper, the remaining egg and cottage cheese, stir well and take off the heat.
4. Divide the dough into 4 pieces, roll each piece, place on the bottom of a ramekin, add spinach filling over dough, place ramekins in your Air Fryer's basket and cook at 360°F for 15 minutes. Serve warm.
5. Enjoy!

Nutrition: cal. 250, fat 12, fiber 2, carbs 23, protein 12

177. Sweet Baby Carrots Dish

Preparation time: 13 minutes **Cooking time:** 10 minutes **Servings:** 4
Ingredients:
- 2 cups baby carrots
- A pinch of salt and black pepper
- 1 tablespoon brown sugar
- ½ tablespoon butter, melted

Directions:
1. In a dish that fits your Air Fryer, mix baby carrots with butter, salt, pepper and sugar, toss, introduce in your Air Fryer and cook at 350°F for 10 minutes.
2. Divide among plates and serve. Enjoy!

Nutrition: calories 100, fat 2, fiber 3, carbs 7, protein 4

179. Zucchini Mix

Preparation time: 10 minutes **Cooking time:** 14 minutes **Servings:** 6
Ingredients:
- 6 zucchinis, halved and then sliced
- Salt and black pepper to the taste
- 1 tablespoon butter
- 1 teaspoon oregano, dried
- ½ cup yellow onion, chopped
- 3 garlic cloves, minced
- 2 ounces parmesan, grated
- ¾ cup heavy cream

Directions:
1. Heat up a pan that fits your Air Fryer with the butter over medium-high heat, add onion, stir and cook for 4 minutes.
2. Add garlic, zucchini, oregano, salt, pepper and heavy cream, toss, introduce in your Air Fryer and cook at 350°F for 10 minutes. Add parmesan, stir, and divide among plates. Enjoy!

Nutrition: calories 160, fat 4, fiber 2, carbs 8, protein 8

DESSERTS

180. Air Fried Apples

Preparation time: 13 minutes **Cooking time:** 17 minutes **Servings:** 4
Ingredients:
- 4 big apples, cored
- A handful of raisins
- 1 tablespoon cinnamon, ground
- Raw honey to the taste

Directions:
1. Fill each apple with raisins, sprinkle cinnamon, drizzle honey, put them in your Air Fryer and cook at 367°F for 17 minutes.
2. Leave them to cool down and serve. Enjoy!

Nutrition: calories 220, fat 3, fiber 4, carbs 6, protein 10

181. Air Fried Bananas

Preparation time: 12 minutes **Cooking time:** 15 minutes **Servings:** 4
Ingredients:
- 3 tablespoons butter
- 2 eggs
- 8 bananas, peeled and halved
- ½ cup cornflour
- 3 tablespoons cinnamon sugar
- 1 cup panko

Directions:
1. Heat a saucepan with the butter over medium-high heat, add the panko, stir and bake for 4 minutes, then transfer to a bowl.
2. Roll them in flour, eggs and panko, place them in your fryer basket, sprinkle with cinnamon sugar and cook at 280°F for 10 minutes.
3. Serve immediately. Enjoy!

Nutrition: calories 165, fat 1, fiber 4, carbs 32, protein 4

182. Berries Mix

Preparation time: 5 minutes **Cooking time:** 6 minutes
Servings: 4
Ingredients:
- 2 tablespoons lemon juice
- 1 and ½ tablespoons maple syrup
- 1 and ½ tablespoons of champagne vinegar
- 1 tablespoon olive oil
- 1-pound strawberries halved
- 1 and ½ cups blueberries
- ¼ cup basil leaves, torn

Directions:
1. In a pan suitable to your Air Fryer, mix lemon juice with maple syrup and vinegar, boil over medium-high heat, add oil, blueberries and strawberries, stir, introduce to your Air Fryer and cook at 310°F for 6 minutes.
2. Sprinkle basil on top and serve! Enjoy!

Nutrition: cal. 163, fat 4, fiber 4, carbs 10, protein 2.1

183. Blueberry Pudding

Preparation time: 14 minutes **Cooking time:** 25 minutes **Servings:** 6
Ingredients:
- 2 cups flour
- 2 cups rolled oats
- 8 cups blueberries
- 1 stick of butter, melted
- 1 cup walnuts, chopped
- 3 tablespoons maple syrup
- 2 tablespoons rosemary, chopped

Directions:
1. Spread blueberries in a greased baking pan and leave aside.
2. Mix rolled oats with the flour, walnuts, butter, maple syrup and rosemary in your food processor, blend well, layer this over blueberries, introduce everything in your Air Fryer and cook in 350°F for 25 minutes.
3. Leave dessert to cool down and cut. Enjoy!

Nutrition: cal. 151, fat 3, fiber 2, carbs 7, protein 4

184. Brown Butter Cookies

Preparation time: 13 minutes **Cooking time:** 10 minutes **Servings:** 6
Ingredients:
- 1 and ½ cups of butter
- 2 cups brown sugar
- 2 eggs, whisked
- 3 cups flour
- 2/3 cup pecans, chopped
- 2 teaspoons vanilla extract
- 1 teaspoon baking soda
- ½ teaspoon baking powder

Directions:
1. Heat a pan with the butter over medium heat, stir until it melts, add brown sugar and stir until it dissolves.
2. Mix flour with pecans, vanilla extract, baking soda, baking powder and eggs and stir well.
3. Add brown butter, stir well and arrange a spoonful of this mix on a lined baking sheet suitable to your air fryer.
4. Introduce in the fryer and cook at 340°F for 10 minutes.
5. Leave cookies to cool down and serve. Enjoy!

Nutrition: calories 144, fat 5, fiber 6, carbs 19, protein 2

185. Carrot Cake

Preparation time: 12 minutes **Cooking time:** 45 minutes **Servings:** 6
Ingredients:
- 5 ounces of flour
- ¾ teaspoon baking powder
- ½ teaspoon baking soda
- ½ teaspoon cinnamon powder
- ¼ teaspoon nutmeg, ground
- ½ teaspoon allspice
- 1 egg
- 3 tablespoons yogurt
- ½ cup sugar
- ¼ cup pineapple juice
- 4 tablespoons sunflower oil
- 1/3 cup carrots, grated
- 1/3 cup pecans, toasted and chopped
- 1/3 cup coconut flakes, shredded
- Cooking spray

Directions:
1. Mix flour with baking soda, powder, salt, allspice, cinnamon, and nutmeg and stir. Combine egg, yogurt, sugar, oil, carrots, pecan pineapple juice and coconut flakes.
2. Mix both blends and mix well. Place it in a springform pan suitable for your air fryer, which you greased with cooking spray.
3. Transfer to your Air Fryer and bake at 320°F for 45 minutes.
4. Leave the cake to cool down, then cut.
5. Enjoy!

Nutrition: cal. 201, fat 6, fiber 20, carbs 22, protein 4

186. Chocolate and Pomegranate Bars

Preparation time: 2 hours **Cooking time:** 10 minutes **Servings:** 6
Ingredients:
- ½ cup milk
- 1 teaspoon vanilla extract
- 1 and ½ cups dark chocolate, chopped
- ½ cup almonds, chopped
- ½ cup pomegranate seeds

Directions:
1. Heat a pan with the milk over medium-low heat, add chocolate, and stir for 5 minutes; remove from the heat and add the vanilla extract, half of the pomegranate seeds and half of the walnuts.
2. Pour this into a lined baking pan, spread, sprinkle a pinch of salt, and the rest of the pomegranate arils and nuts, introduce in your Air Fryer and cook at 300°F for 4 minutes.
3. Store in the refrigerator for 2 hours before serving.
4. Enjoy!

Nutrition: calories 68, fat 1, fiber 4, carbs 6, protein 1

187. Chocolate Cake

Preparation time: 13 minutes **Cooking time:** 30 minutes **Servings:** 12
Ingredients:
- ¾ cup white flour
- ¾ cup whole wheat flour
- 1 teaspoon baking soda
- ¾ teaspoon pumpkin pie spice
- ¾ cup sugar
- 1 banana, mashed
- ½ teaspoon baking powder
- 2 tablespoons canola oil
- ½ cup Greek yogurt
- 8 ounces of canned pumpkin puree
- Cooking spray
- 1 egg
- ½ teaspoon vanilla extract
- 2/3 cup chocolate chips

Directions:
1. Combine white flour with whole wheat flour, salt, baking soda, powder and pumpkin spices.
2. Blend the sugar with the oil, banana, yogurt, pumpkin purée, vanilla and egg and stir with a mixer.
3. Combine the two mixes, add the chocolate chips, stir and pour into a greased Bundt mold that fits your fryer. Place in your air fryer and cook at 330 °F for 30 minutes.
4. Let the cake cool, cut and serve. Enjoy!

Nutrition: calories 233, fat 7, fiber 7, carbs 29, protein 4

188. Cinnamon Rolls and Cream Cheese Dip

Preparation time: 2 hours **Cooking time:** 17 minutes
Servings: 8
Ingredients:
- 1 pound bread dough
- ¾ cup brown sugar
- 1 and ½ tablespoons cinnamon, ground
- ¼ cup butter, melted

For the cream cheese dip:
- 2 tablespoons butter
- 4 ounces of cream cheese
- 1 and ¼ cups of sugar
- ½ teaspoon vanilla

Directions:
1. Roll the pastry onto a floured work surface, shape it into a rectangle and brush with 1/4 cup of butter.
2. In a bowl, combine the cinnamon with the sugar, toss, and sprinkle over the dough. Roll the dough into a round, seal well and cut it into eight pieces.
3. Let the rolls stand for 2 hours, put them in your fryer basket, cook at 350°F for 5 minutes, then turn them over.
4. Bake for another 4 minutes and transfer to a tray. Blend the cream cheese with the butter, sugar and vanilla and beat well.
5. Serve your cinnamon buns with this creamy cheese dip. Enjoy!

Nutrition: calories 201, fat 1, fiber 0, carbs 5, protein 6

189. Cocoa Cake

Preparation time: 13 minutes **Cooking time:** 17 minutes **Servings:** 6
Ingredients:
- 3 eggs
- 3 ounces of sugar
- 3.5 ounces butter, melted
- 1 teaspoon cocoa powder
- 3 ounces of flour
- ½ teaspoon lemon juice

Directions:
1. Mix 1 tablespoon of butter with cocoa powder and whisk. Stir the remaining butter into the sugar, eggs, flour and lemon juice.
2. Beat well and pour half into a cake pan that suits your fryer. Add half of the cocoa blend, spread, add the remaining layer of butter and top with the remaining cocoa powder.
3. Place in your air fryer and cook at 360°F for 17 minutes.
4. Refrigerate the cake before slicing. Enjoy!

Nutrition: cal. 340, fat 11, fiber 3, carbs 25, protein 5

190. Easy Granola

Preparation time: 13 minutes **Cooking time:** 35 minutes **Servings:** 4
Ingredients:
- 1 cup coconut, shredded
- ½ cup almonds
- ½ cup pecans, chopped
- 2 tablespoons sugar
- ½ cup pumpkin seeds
- ½ cup sunflower seeds
- 2 tablespoons sunflower oil
- 1 teaspoon nutmeg, ground
- 1 teaspoon of apple pie spice mix

Directions:
1. Mix almonds and pecans with pumpkin seeds, sunflower seeds, coconut, nutmeg and apple pie spice mix and stir well.
2. Heat a pan with the oil over medium heat, add sugar and stir well.
3. Pour it over the nuts and coconut mix and stir well.
4. Spread this on a lined baking sheet that fits your Air Fryer, introduce it to your Air Fryer, cook at 300°F and bake for 25 minutes.
5. Leave your granola to cool down and cut.
6. Enjoy!

Nutrition: calories 322, fat 7, fiber 8, carbs 12, protein 7

191. Figs and Coconut Butter Mix

Preparation time: 6 minutes **Cooking time:** 4 minutes
Servings: 3
Ingredients:
- 2 tablespoons coconut butter
- 12 figs, halved
- ¼ cup sugar
- 1 cup almonds, toasted and chopped

Directions:
1. Put butter in a pan that fits your Air Fryer and melt over medium-high heat.
2. Add figs, sugar and almonds, toss, introduce in your Air Fryer and cook at 300°F for 4 minutes.
3. Divide into bowls and serve cold. Enjoy!

Nutrition: calories 170, fat 4, fiber 5, carbs 7, protein 9

192. Ginger Cheesecake

Preparation time: 2 hours and 10 minutes **Cooking time:** 20 minutes **Servings:** 6
Ingredients:
- 2 teaspoons butter, melted
- ½ cup ginger cookies, crumbled
- 16 ounces of cream cheese, soft
- 2 eggs
- ½ cup sugar
- 1 teaspoon rum
- ½ teaspoon vanilla extract
- ½ teaspoon nutmeg, ground

Directions:
1. Grease a pan with the butter and spread cookie crumbs on the bottom.
2. In a bowl, beat cream cheese with nutmeg, vanilla, rum and eggs, whisk well and spread over the cookie crumbs.
3. Introduce in your Air Fryer and cook at 340°F for 20 minutes.
4. Leave the cheesecake to cool down and keep it in the fridge for 2 hours before slicing. Enjoy!

Nutrition: cal. 412, fat 12, fiber 6, carbs 20, protein 6

193. Lemon Bars

Preparation time: 11 minutes **Cooking time:** 25 minutes **Servings:** 6
Ingredients:
- 4 eggs
- 2 and ¼ cups flour
- Juice from 2 lemons
- 1 cup butter, soft
- 2 cups sugar

Directions:
1. Mix butter with ½ cup sugar and 2 cups flour, stir well, press on the bottom of a pan that fits your Air Fryer, introduce it into the fryer and bake at 350°F for 10 minutes.
2. In another bowl, mix the rest of the sugar with the rest of the flour, eggs and lemon juice, whisk well and spread over the crust.
3. Introduce in the fryer at 350°F for 15 minutes more and leave aside to cool down, cut bars and serve them. Enjoy!

Nutrition: calories 125, fat 4, fiber 4, carbs 16, protein 2

194. Lime Cheesecake

Preparation time: 4 hours and 10 minutes **Cooking time:** 4 minutes **Servings:** 10
Ingredients:
- 2 tablespoons butter, melted
- 2 teaspoons of sugar
- 4 ounces of flour
- ¼ cup coconut, shredded

For the filling:
- 1 pound cream cheese
- Zest from 1 lime, grated
- Juice from 1 lime
- 2 cups hot water
- 2 sachets of lime jelly

Directions:
1. Mix coconut with flour, butter and sugar, stir well and press this on the bottom of a pan that fits your Air Fryer.
2. Meanwhile, put the hot water in a bowl, add jelly sachets and stir until it dissolves.
3. Put cream cheese in a bowl, add jelly, lime juice and zest and whisk well.
4. Add this over the crust, spread, introduce to the Air Fryer and bake at 300°F for 4 minutes.
5. Keep in the fridge for 4 hours before serving.

Nutrition: calories 260, fat 23, fiber 2, carbs 5, protein 7

195. Macaroons

Preparation time: 10 minutes **Cooking time:** 8 minutes
Servings: 20
Ingredients:
- 2 tablespoons sugar
- 4 egg whites
- 2 cups coconut, shredded
- 1 teaspoon vanilla extract

Directions:
1. Mix egg whites with stevia and beat with a mixer.

2. Add coconut and vanilla extract, whisk again, shape small balls out of this mix, introduce them to your Air Fryer and cook at 340°F for 8 minutes. Serve macaroons cold. Enjoy!

Nutrition: calories 55, fat 6, fiber 1, carbs 2, protein 1

196. Pumpkin Pie

Preparation time: 14 minutes **Cooking time:** 15 minutes **Servings:** 9

Ingredients:
- 1 tablespoon sugar
- 2 tablespoons flour
- 1 tablespoon butter
- 2 tablespoons water

For the pumpkin pie filling:
- 3.5 ounces of pumpkin flesh, chopped
- 1 teaspoon nutmeg
- 1 teaspoon mixed spice
- 3 ounces of water
- 1 egg, whisked
- 1 tablespoon sugar

Directions:
1. Put three ounces of water in a pot. Bring to a boil on medium heat; add pumpkin, egg, 1 tablespoon sugar, spice and nutmeg, stir, boil for 20 minutes, take off the heat and blend using an immersion blender.
2. Mix flour with butter, 1 tablespoon of sugar and 2 tablespoons of water and knead your dough.
3. Grease a pie pan that fits your Air Fryer with butter, press dough into the pan, fill with pumpkin pie filling, place in your Air Fryer's basket and cook at 360°F for 15 minutes.
4. Slice and serve warm. Enjoy!

Nutrition: calories 200, fat 5, fiber 2, carbs 5, protein 6

197. Simple Cheesecake

Preparation time: 14 minutes **Cooking time:** 15 minutes **Servings:** 15

Ingredients:
- 1 pound cream cheese
- ½ teaspoon vanilla extract
- 2 eggs
- 4 tablespoons sugar
- 1 cup graham crackers, crumbled
- 2 tablespoons butter

Directions:
1. In a bowl, mix crackers with butter.
2. Press crackers mix on the bottom of a lined cake pan, introduce in your Air Fryer and cook at 350°F for 4 minutes.
3. Meanwhile, mix sugar with cream cheese, eggs and vanilla and whisk well.
4. Spread filling over crackers crust and cook your cheesecake in your Air Fryer at 310°F for 15 minutes. Leave cake in the fridge for 3 hours, slice and serve. Enjoy!

Nutrition: cal. 245, fat 12, fiber 1, carbs 20, protein 3

198. Special Brownies

Preparation time: 12 minutes **Cooking time:** 17 minutes **Servings:** 4

Ingredients:
- 1 egg
- 1/3 cup cocoa powder
- 1/3 cup sugar
- 7 tablespoons butter
- ½ teaspoon vanilla extract
- ¼ cup white flour
- ¼ cup walnuts, chopped
- ½ teaspoon baking powder
- 1 tablespoon peanut butter

Directions:
1. Heat a pan with 6 tablespoons of butter and the sugar on medium heat, stir, and bake for 5 minutes. Transfer this to a bowl, add salt, vanilla extract, cocoa powder, egg, baking powder, walnuts and flour, stir the whole thing well and pour into a pan that fits your Air Fryer.
2. Mix 1 tablespoon butter with peanut butter, heat up in your microwave for a few seconds, stir well and drizzle this over the brownies mix.
3. Introduce in your Air Fryer, bake at 320°F and bake for 17 minutes.
4. Leave brownies to cool down and cut. Enjoy!

Nutrition: calories 223, fat 32, fiber 1, carbs 3, protein 6

199. Tasty Orange Cookies

Preparation time: 13 minutes **Cooking time:** 12 minutes **Servings:** 8

Ingredients:
- 2 cups flour
- 1 teaspoon baking powder

- ½ cup butter, soft
- ¾ cup sugar
- 1 egg, whisked
- 1 teaspoon vanilla extract
- 1 tablespoon orange zest, grated

For the filling:
- 4 ounces of cream cheese, soft
- ½ cup butter
- 2 cups powdered sugar

Directions:
1. Mix cream cheese with ½ cup butter and 2 cups powdered sugar; stir well using your mixer and leave aside for now.
2. In another bowl, mix flour with baking powder.
3. Mix ½ cup butter with ¾ cup sugar, egg, vanilla extract and orange zest n a third bowl, and whisk well.
4. Combine flour with the orange mix, stir well and scoop 1 tablespoon of the mix on a lined baking sheet that fits your air fryer.
5. Repeat with the rest of the orange batter, introduce it to the fryer and cook at 340°F for 12 minutes.
6. Leave cookies to cool down, spread cream filling on half the top with the other cookies and serve. Enjoy!

Nutrition: calories 124, fat 5, fiber 6, carbs 8, protein 4

200. Tomato Cake

Preparation time: 14 minutes **Cooking time:** 30 minutes **Servings:** 4

Ingredients:
- 1 and ½ cups flour
- 1 teaspoon cinnamon powder
- 1 teaspoon baking powder
- 1 teaspoon baking soda
- ¾ cup maple syrup
- 1 cup chopped tomatoes
- ½ cup olive oil
- 2 tablespoons apple cider vinegar

Directions:
1. Mix flour with baking powder, soda, cinnamon and maple syrup and stir well.
2. Mix tomatoes with olive oil and vinegar and stir well.
3. Combine the 2 mixtures, stir well, pour into a greased round pan that fits your Air Fryer, introduce into the fryer and cook at 360°F for 30 minutes.
4. Leave the cake to cool down, and slice. Enjoy!

Nutrition: calories 153, fat 2, fiber 1, carbs 25, protein 4

CONCLUSION

Owning an air fryer is a big decision. Nobody will buy anything they don't need. But it doesn't have to be tricky because there are so many advantages to owning an air fryer that you wouldn't have imagined until you bought one. You will soon make all sorts of good food in your fryer, and I can guarantee that if you try to use it, you will not regret the decision.

Printed in Great Britain
by Amazon